SHAMANOMICS

A Short Guide
to the
Failure, Fallacies
and Future of
Macroeconomics

Giles Conway-Gordon

outskirts
press

Outskirts Press, Inc.
http://www.outskirtspress.com

Paperback ISBN: 978-1-9772-2685-3
Hardback ISBN: 978-1-9772-3910-5

Outskirts Press and the "OP" logo are trademarks belonging to Outskirts Press, Inc.

PRINTED IN THE UNITED STATES OF AMERICA

For my mother and father

TABLE OF CONTENTS

Introduction. i

Chapter 1: 1982-2008: The Golden Age 1

Chapter 2: The Crisis of 2008 12

Chapter 3: Whose Fault Was It? Who Saw It Coming?. 30

Chapter 4: What Went Wrong? Postmortems and Lessons 54

Chapter 5: What are Macroeconomists For?. 65

Chapter 6: Mathematics: Was Keynes A Muggle ? 79

Chapter 7: Theories, Models and Orthodoxies 101

Chapter 8: Multiple Universes, Economics T.O.E. 131

Chapter 9: Blinded by Non-Science. 137

Chapter 10: The Pretence of Wisdom:
          The Nobel Economics Prize 152

Chapter 11: Dentists, Engineers, Plumbers and Novelists. 163

Chapter 12: Where do we Go From Here? - Back to the Future . 170

Epilogue: The Corona Virus. 182

Bibliography. 184

Index 189

INTRODUCTION

In 2008 all of our models failed - all, across the board.

> **Alan Greenspan**, former Chairman, Federal Reserve Bank of the USA, on CNBC, October 7th, 2011.

Most macroeconomics of the past 30 years has been spectacularly useless at best and positively harmful at worst.

> **Paul Krugman**, Lionel Robbins lecture at the London School of Economics, June 10th, 2009.

I have been increasingly moved to wonder whether my job is a job or a racket, whether economists, and particularly economic theorists, may not be in the position that Cicero ascribed to the augurs of Rome – that they should cover their faces or burst into laughter when they meet in the street.

> **Frank Knight**, Presidential address to the American Economic Association, 1950, quoted by Ronald Coase (winner of the Nobel Prize in Economics, 1991) in his 'Essays on Economics and Economists'.

Why did nobody see it coming?

> **Queen Elizabeth II**, visiting the London School of Economics, November 4th, 2008.

To allow the market mechanism to be sole director of the fate of human beings and their natural environment ...... would result in the demolition of society.

> **Karl Polanyi**, The Great Transformation, 1944.

Her Majesty's question was a good one and it is still, more than 10 years after the event, unanswered. How is it that the worst crisis to hit the global economic and financial system since the Great Depression of the 1920-30s was not foreseen by the world's central bankers and finance ministers and by the vast army of economists working in those institutions and in Academia?

There is a second question, which follows naturally from the first. It is: why is it that the recovery of the global economy from the Crisis has taken so long and has been so weak, in spite of the enormous monetary stimulus supplied by the central banks of the developed economies. This prolonged weakness is not supposed to happen. It directly contradicts the preferred macroeconomic model used by the Federal Reserve in the USA, by the central banks of most of the other major developed economies and by their finance ministries.

The central tenet of this theory says that economies are inherently self-balancing: if economies are left to themselves, the natural operation of the free market will ensure that they will return automatically to stable equilibrium. Furthermore, recessions can always be avoided by simply increasing the money supply and lowering interest rates, leading to increased demand and consumption and increased capital investment by companies, generating a reliable virtuous circle, ensuring a return to a desirable equilibrium of renewed growth, falling unemployment and a renewed rise in living standards.

This, very obviously, has not happened. Growth rates in the developed economies and across the globe (with the possible, and possibly temporary, exception of the USA) are significantly below their long-term average - and until recently were even in some cases negative - and debt, both private and public, is at unprecedented levels and continues to grow. Thus, the Economics 'profession' has failed twice over:

first, in failing to foresee the risk of, and to take steps to prevent, the catastrophe of the 2008 Crisis and, secondly, in failing to deliver a rapid recovery to durable growth, a recovery which, according to their models, should have been all the faster and stronger given the depth of the preceding recession and the unprecedented monetary stimulus applied to cure it.

Yet the architects of the Crisis and of its now very lengthy troubled aftermath - not only those immediately responsible for it like **Alan Greenspan, Lawrence Summers** and **Robert Rubin**, and Alan Greenspan's successor as Chairman of the United States Federal Reserve, **Ben Bernanke**, but the numerous macroeconomics pundits like **Paul Krugman** and **Joseph Stiglitz** (many of them, interestingly, winners of the Nobel Economics Prize) and the economists in the global economic institutions like the IMF and the World Bank at the time of the Crisis - continue to utter complacent, regretful musings on the pervasive low economic growth in the global economy and its failure to return to historic growth rates.

Much worse, they continue to receive universal respect and attention. In spite of the catastrophic failure of their profession, macroeconomists have never had it so good. This is utterly undeserved. The Crisis comprehensively discredited not simply those immediately responsible for the debacle but the entire basis of any claim by economists to professional and intellectual authority and social usefulness.

In the last few years the slow processes of the law have resulted in enormous fines being paid by the banks whose uncontrolled activities triggered the Crisis, with more than $320 billion extracted from them. Yes, the conduct of the banks was undoubtedly reprehensible (and in some cases criminal) but the architects of the Crisis – Alan Greenspan, Lawrence Summers, Robert Rubin and their successors like Ben

Bernanke - who were responsible for the regime of unfettered monetary free-for-all which led to the Crisis, are still enjoying life as free men.

Even more deplorably, their comments and articles on the persisting dismal consequences of the Crisis continue to receive ready acceptance in the media and in the pages of respected and influential journals like the Financial Times, the New York Times and the Economist. The US Federal Inquiry of January, 2011, concluded that the Crisis was clearly foreseeable. So far from continuing to bask in widespread public respect, these 'experts' should have been called to severe account for their comprehensive failure to discharge their principal fiduciary duty: the maintenance of financial and economic stability.

The US financial markets were the epicenter of the 2008 Crisis. Ten years earlier, the Far Eastern crisis of 1998 and the ensuing Russian default had given rise to widespread panic in global financial markets which had been resolved in large part because of the global influence and calm persuasion of Greenspan, Summers and Rubin. At the time, in an adulatory article entitled 'The Three Marketeers' in its issue of February 15th, 1999, TIME magazine described these three as 'The Committee to Save the World'. Most unfortunately, this uncritical faith in the omniscience and competence of these three and of their colleagues in the macroeconomics business still persists.

Now that there is some more reflective distance from the 2008 Crisis and the actions - and lack of action - that triggered it have been well identified and analyzed, how is it that these guilty men managed to avoid even a limited calling-to-account for their failure? So far from discreetly retiring from public life and vanishing into deserved obscurity they continue to pursue full and public professional lives very much as before.

Yet behind their failure lay another much more serious and fundamental failure – a failure which has comprehensively discredited almost the entire Economics profession. It was the failure of the dominant macroeconomic model long preferred by the financial authorities in most of the world and in much of Academia – the so-called Dynamic Stochastic General Equilibrium model. It was uncritical acceptance of this theory on the part of the world's central banks and finance ministries, acting on the recommendations of their Economics advisers, that was the origin of the policy errors which led directly to the Crisis. It is macroeconomists, therefore, who bear the main responsibility for it.

Many books have been written explaining the Crisis, most of them by economists for economists, or at least for those with a reasonable grounding in the opaque language used by economists. As fully paid-up members of the Economics profession, many of the authors of these books have tended to exercise a considerable measure of professional etiquette and have down-played criticism of their professional colleagues. Fortunately, there have been admirable exceptions to this kid-glove treatment in the shape of the Cassandras who predicted the Crisis and those few commentators who delivered deservedly harsh criticism of the performance of the 'experts' whose dereliction of duty led to it.

This book is intended as a short personal take on and guide to the failures and fallacies of the Economics profession and economists, and particularly of the so-called macroeconomists, those who specialize in studying the interaction of the major factors which make up a developed economy - employment, growth, interest rates, inflation etc. - and who play a prominent role in advising governments and formulating the policies of central banks and finance ministries. It is also a criticism of the excessive and, on the basis of the evidence, mostly disastrous influence which macroeconomists have wielded and continue to wield and of the utterly unwarranted respect they still continue to enjoy.

Finally, I look at the future of macroeconomics and the growing evidence in the work of a few economists and social thinkers that the main thrust of macroeconomic thinking is undergoing a decisive, welcome and overdue shift away from opaque abstraction towards engagement with the real world. Importantly this shift is also a shift from socially unuseful, even dangerous, theorizing towards a concern with the real welfare of real human beings. In this, Economics is, after the two-hundred-and-fifty-year unrestrained dominance of the free market, returning to moral and social roots it should never have left.

Although my arguments apply to macroeconomics and macroeconomists in general, most of the focus is on the US economy and on the US Economics profession. The reason is not only that the US financial markets were the epicenter of the Crisis and that the US has a dominant role in the global economy, its policy actions reverberating throughout the world, but that the US dominates the Economics industry, not only in the numbers of practicing economists but also in academic Economics and in the formulation of the economic theories and models which central banks and ministries of finance around the world use to manage their countries' economies.

I am hopeful that this book can find a readership outside Economics and the finance industry. I have therefore used plain language and kept to the KISS principle; there is no mathematics. My aim has been to present simply the main themes of my argument but to include references to the many relevant sources to enable those wishing to delve more deeply into specific aspects of the saga to do so.

The macroeconomic 'specialists' have had a ringside seat in the arena of economic theory and practice and in the financial markets for several decades (indeed - and this is part of the problem - large numbers of them participate as a sort of tag team in the Economics policy ring, moving in and out of official positions as advisers to governments from Academia or the finance industry). As noted above, their influence has been mostly malign, not to say disastrous, and the victims of the failure and errors of the Economics 'profession' include a large proportion of the global population.

In truth, the experience of the last few decades and of the Crisis itself has provided conclusive proof that Economics is not and can never be a true science. The macroeconomists, self-appointed masters of the Economics universe, have proven to be little better than witch-doctors – shamans, pretending to a wisdom and expertise which they clearly don't have, uttering their ritualistic mumbo-jumbo and issuing forecasts and urging policy recommendations which mostly turn out to be not only badly inaccurate and misguided but, as the Crisis demonstrated, very dangerous.

At last however several recent works indicate that macroeconomics is starting to shift its focus from the vacuous 'angels-on-the-head-of-a-pin' theorizing which has absorbed the 'profession' for the last 70 years and to concern itself with the real welfare of real human beings. It is not a moment too soon.

∿∿

Chapter 1: **The Golden Age. Part 1: The Golden Age of Growth** and **Part 2: The Golden Age of Macroeconomics - We Did It!** sets the scene, with the strong steady growth of the 1980s and '90s stimulating a parallel boom in the size, prestige, influence and self-esteem of the Economics 'profession'.

Chapter 2: **The Crisis of 2008. Part 1: Origins and Causes,** summarizes the major causes of the Crisis - uncontrolled credit, flawed risk assessment and extreme financial interdependency. **Part 2: Effects** and **Consequences,** describes the Crisis and its short- and long-term effects: immediate global collapse followed by persistent stagnation, sky-high debt and policy impotence.

Chapter 3: **Whose Fault was It? Who Saw it Coming?,** identifies the guilty parties and policies, including regulatory failure, a mistaken belief in unregulated free markets and the fundamental failure of the dominant economic model used by the US Federal Reserve and the world's finance ministries and central banks. **We Didn't Do It!** notes the 'we're not guilty' arguments of the main culprits. **Who Saw it Coming?** identifies the few who did see it coming.

Chapter 4: **What went Wrong?: Postmortems and Lessons** reviews the postmortem and 'non mea culpa' literature and the series of post-Crisis high-level conferences which have considered both the Crisis and its still-developing consequences for macroeconomic thinking and policy.

Chapter 5: **What Are Macroeconomists For?** questions the social use and purpose of macroeconomists. It looks at the policy advice process and the need for forecasts - through which economists come to influence the policies pursued by governments - and the shortcomings of the forecasting 'science'.

Chapter 6: **Mathematics: Was Keynes a Muggle?** describes the annexation of Economics by mathematics, the flaws and failings of some of the abstract mathematical procedures used by economists and the confidence-trick consequence of this invasion. But at last: **No more smoke and mirrors - Paul Romer**'s paper skewering the malign mathematical domination of Economics.

Chapter 7: **Theories, Models and Orthodoxies** looks at economic theorizing and analyses the inherent fallacies of the models on which economists base their forecasts and their policy recommendations. It also notes the process by which particular theories devised by particular economists for particular circumstances acquire the status of dogmatic orthodoxies, with alternative theories derided and suppressed. The origins, features and shortcomings of the dominant DSGE (Dynamic Stochastic General Equilibrium) model are described. The Fed's suppression of dissident macroeconomic theories is noted.

Chapter 8: **Multiple Economic Universes, Economics T.O.E.** discusses the multiplicity of conflicting and contradictory macroeconomic theories.

Chapter 9: **Blinded by Non-Science**, disputes the claim that Economics is a 'hard' science, comparable to physics or chemistry, and describes the flawed use of statistics by economists. The contribution of **Behavioral Economics** is assessed.

Chapter 10: **The Pretence of Wisdom: the Nobel Prize in Economics** discusses the unfortunate endorsement effect of the Nobel Economics Prize for the Economics 'profession' and considers the minor real significance of most prizewinners' contributions.

Chapter 11: **Dentists, Engineers, Plumbers and Novelists**, discusses the various analogies for Economics which have been proposed, from Keynes' dentists to Shiller's engineers. Given the infinitely variable nature of economic behavior, economists should more accurately be viewed as novelists.

Chapter 12: **Where do we Go from Here?: Back to the Future** looks at the encouraging signs that Economics is, at last, returning to moral and social considerations which it should never have abandoned.

Conclusion: On the evidence of their track-record, macroeconomists have proved themselves to be no better than shamans and witchdoctors.

It is therefore high time for the respect still universally accorded to economists, and in particular to macroeconomists, to cease.

~~~

Epilogue: The Corona Virus. This book was written before the onset of the Corona-19 virus. The virus is inducing a worldwide economic recession. Although the criticism levelled at macroeconomics in the book needs no qualification, macroeconomic theorizing is for the time being irrelevant. Longer-term, however, the virus is likely to reinforce the discrediting of the free market/growth-at-all-costs paradigm and to herald a seismic change in the structure and operation of developed economies, with lower but more equitable growth, a greater attention to industrial and social security of all kinds and, finally, a better relationship with the natural world. In this environment it will be no less necessary to scrutinize critically the theories and policy recommendations of macroeconomists.

Chapter 1

1982-2008: The Golden Age

PART 1: THE GOLDEN AGE OF GROWTH

During more than two decades, from 1982 to 2007, the US economy and the World economy enjoyed a golden age of unprecedented sustained growth with low inflation. This exceptional growth and stability came as a welcome change after the disastrous economic experience of the 1970s. In 1970, **President Nixon**, facing re-election in 1972, had taken the US$ off the gold standard and appointed **Arthur Burns** as Chairman of the Federal Reserve with instructions to stimulate the US economy. The result, with a bit of help from the quadrupling of the oil price after the OPEC embargo in 1974, was a severe recession, with inflation and unemployment both rising above 10%. Unemployment finally hit a high of 10.8% in December, 1982.

In 1979, **Paul Volcker** was appointed Chairman of the Fed by **Jimmy Carter**. His severely restrictive monetary regime, though very unpopular at the time, restored the US economy to health. Inflation fell steadily, laying the groundwork for a Golden Age of Growth. This golden age of growth was matched by a parallel golden age in the US Stock Market; the Dow rose from a low of 776.92 in 1982 to 13,264.82 at the close of 2007.

Besides the strong action taken by Paul Volcker, several other factors contributed to the unprecedented gains in growth and in the financial markets during this period (and also to the steady decline in the rate of inflation). First, the pace of the IT revolution accelerated, generating a surge in productivity in the US, the economy of its birth. The enormous increase in computing bang-for-the-buck, expressed in Moore's law, helped to double US productivity from its level in the 1980s to 2005.[1]

Secondly, the volume of world trade expanded strongly, helping to generate a surge in the growth of the global economy. The principle of free trade and the avoidance of protectionism was a key element in the global trade architecture adopted by the institutions set up by the major economic nations after the Second World War - the IMF, the General Agreement on Tariffs and Trade (GATT) and the World Trade Organization (WTO), which succeeded GATT in 1995.

The free-trade principle reflected the universal recognition that the recession of the late 1920s had metastasized into the Great Depression in large part due to the misguided resort to protectionism by the USA (Smoot-Hawley) and the other major trading nations. As the global economy recovered from World War II, national economies picked up and nations resumed trading with each other. This trend accelerated steadily: global exports of goods and services as a proportion of global GDP rose from 22.4% to 32.7% over the period from 1980 to 2008, with trade growth expanding at nearly twice the rate of GDP.[2]

Another important factor contributing to the global expansion was the steady reduction in geo-political tension during the Golden Age. The Cold War between the USA (as leader of the western democracies) and the USSR had brought the world to the brink of open conflict with the Cuban missile crisis of 1963. Yet in 1990 the Soviet Union, unable to keep up the pretense of economic strength any longer, collapsed, along with the Berlin Wall, and democratic capitalism became the dominant economic and political system of the world. The removal of this major source of tension and uncertainty provided a solid geopolitical underpinning to the accelerating, growth-enhancing flows of trade and investment between the world's nations.

One of the positive consequences of this détente was the emergence of the larger developing countries - Brazil, India and China, with Russia as a lesser member – to become significant trading nations and serious participants in the global economy, as producers of natural resources, as consumers and as recipients of foreign direct investment capital.

A second, very positive, consequence of this growth was a fall, unprecedented in human history in its wide extent and size, in the proportion of the world's population living in extreme poverty (reckoned in 1995 to be an income of less than US$1 per day, now $1.90). Much of this fall was attributable to the explosive growth of China but the effect was widespread. It has continued since, with Africa now taking up the growth baton. According to updated Oxfam figures the proportion of the world's population living in extreme poverty has halved over the past 15 years from 36% to 18%.

There were a few hiccups along the way - some of the Far Eastern countries got into debt difficulties in 1998 arising from ill-conceived currency policies and Russia defaulted on its debt in the same year - but the steady positive trend of stronger growth in an open global economy was not derailed.

Thus the global political and economic landscape seemed increasingly to confirm the spreading victory of liberal, democratic capitalism. The theories of **Francis Fukuyama** and **Thomas Friedman**, set out in their books, **'The End of History'** and **'The World is Flat'**, proclaiming the final victory of liberal capitalist democracy as the prevailing political system under which humanity would henceforth live, met with almost universal agreement.

Chapter 1, Part 1: Notes

1. Report by National Bureau of Economic Research, March, 2010.
2. Sources: IMF, WTO, UNCTAD.

PART 2: THE GOLDEN AGE OF MACROECONOMICS: WE DID IT!

'The central problem of depression-prevention has been solved, for all practical purposes...' **Robert Lucas**, winner of the Nobel Economics Prize in 1995, in his address, January, 2003, as the Association's President, to the American Economic Association.

'Economic science had solved the great problems of recession and depression ... monetary and fiscal policy could get us out of almost any hole .... and as an added dividend both monetary and fiscal policy could even be fine-tuned to engineer permanently low unemployment and permanently high output.' **George Akerlof** and **Robert Shiller**, describing the professional confidence of **Paul Samuelson**, in **Animal Spirits,** February, 2010.

'The state of macro[economics] is good.' **Olivier Blanchard**, then at MIT, later Chief Economist at the IMF, in a paper on **The Future of Macroeconomics**, August, 2008.

Hand-in-hand with the Golden Age of economic growth flourished a parallel Golden Age: a Golden Age for economists and in particular for macroeconomists, those responsible for defining and shaping the economic policies followed by governments. As the global economy grew strongly and steadily during the 25 years after the inflationary 1970s and stock markets across the world racked up continuous 15% p.a. gains, the Economics profession enjoyed a parallel spectacular expansion. As the positive effects of what has come to be called the Great Moderation spread, its golden aura radiated ever more widely to envelop and stimulate the entire Economics profession, in Academia, in finance and business and in the media.

Academia

In Academia the major universities offering degrees in Economics, saw their student enrolments soar. Between 1980 and 2005, the numbers of undergraduates taking Economics as a major at the leading Economics colleges (**Yale, Harvard, MIT, Princeton, Chicago**) more than doubled. There was a parallel explosion in the numbers of students selecting finance (including financial mathematics, model-building and number-crunching) as their degree course.[1]

Finance and Business

At the same time, as the influence of the Economics profession grew, it became essential, for banks and major corporations with any ambition to being considered competent and up-to-date, to create and/or expand departments dedicated to economic analysis. These departments served a dual purpose: they were not only a demonstration of a commitment to competent analysis with the aim of improving the management of their institutions and of their clients' businesses and investments[2], they also acted as effective publicity for their companies via exposure on television and other media channels. Correspondingly, the demand for Economics graduates with the appropriate academic qualifications soared.

The Financial Media

As the Great Moderation progressed this demand was given a further strong boost by the creation and explosive growth of media coverage of the world's financial markets, particularly on television. **CNBC**, offering continuous reporting and comment on the US and global financial markets, was launched in April, 1989. The channel added Asian coverage in 1995 and European in 1996. **Bloomberg TV**, an extension of the globally-dominant data-analysis terminal service used by financial market professionals, was launched in January, 1997.

Between them these networks now have more than 500 million subscribers worldwide and deliver informed comment on developments in the global economy and geopolitics (plus, in the case of Bloomberg, a comprehensive analytical database for market professionals) on an effective 24 hour-per-day basis. In April, 1994, the Guide to the World Wide Web, created by Jerry Yang and David Filo and providing real-time stock- and news-monitoring geared mainly to individual private investors, was renamed **Yahoo**. The company went public in April, 1996 and the stock went up more than 15 times in less than 4 years.

Global financial markets had for some while been operating on a virtual 24-hour schedule during the business week, with the major banks and financial institutions present in Hong Kong, Singapore or Tokyo in the Far East, in London in the European time-zone and in New York in the USA. Thus an institution's trading book could be handed over from the Far Eastern markets to London and Europe and then to New York in the course of the global business day.

The matching 24-hours-per-day media coverage of global financial markets generated a corresponding continuous demand for content. Professional economists, both in Academia and in the major financial institutions, found themselves in great demand for views and informed comment on developments in the financial markets, on official financial data releases, on government policy and on the market reactions to all these items.[3]

The Political Angle

Politicians have always needed guidance in their management of the economies of their countries, since most of them have little or no experience of business, let alone Economics. In the past, before the ascendancy and spread of Economics, the economic advice available to governments was limited, reflecting the primitive state of economic thinking. The Great Depression of the 1920s and '30s and the devastation and human misery it caused led to an intense focus on the need to identify both the reasons for the crisis and possible solutions to the wretched conditions it produced. It was as a reaction and response to the human misery of the Great Depression that **John Maynard Keynes** wrote his great work **'The General Theory of Employment, Interest and Money'**. His book, published in 1936, has come to be regarded as the foundation of macroeconomics.

Professional Associations and Economics Journals

The explosive growth in the Economics business during the last few decades of the last century was also reflected in the parallel rise in two other indicators: membership of Economics professional bodies and associations and the number and range of the professional journals devoted to Economics and, later, to specialized subsidiary branches of the subject.

- **Professional Associations**

The premier US association for professional economists, the American Economic Association, was formed in 1885. The explosive growth in the number of professional economists, both in Academia and in business and finance saw its numbers triple from 6,936 in 1950 to 21,578 in 1990. During the years following the World War II, the continued growth in the range and influence of Economics led to a similar increase both in the creation of associations specializing in sub-branches of Economics and in their membership numbers.

- **Economics Journals**

The growth in Economics over the last 60 years also led to an explosion in the number of professional journals dedicated to the 'science'.

Much earlier the **American Economic Association** had published an economic journal in 1886. The Association then launched Economic and Quarterly Bulletins in 1908 and in 1911 absorbed these into the **American Economic Review**, probably the most respected and influential of the now very large number of professional Economics journals.

Econometrica, the journal of the Econometric Society, formed in December, 1930 with a rollcall of the most eminent economists of the day as founders and early members (Keynes, Pigou, Lionel Robbins, etc.), was launched in 1933. Other early Economics journals include: the **Economic Journal** (1891), the **Journal of Political Economy** (1892), the **Quarterly Journal of Economics**, (1886), the **Review of Economics and Statistics** (1919) and the **Review of Economic Studies** (1933). Judged by the frequency of citations of articles in these journals, these are the most authoritative professional Economics journals but there are many others.[4]

In the decades after World War II the number of professional Economics journals proliferated in parallel with the explosive growth of the subject in Academia and in government, finance and business. JSTOR, the digital library of academic and specialist journals, formed in 1995 to facilitate digital access to professional periodicals by academic institutions worldwide, now lists 166 journals under the heading 'Economics', most of them launched from 1960 onwards.

A study of the journals launched since 1960 shows the increasing specialization of Economics and confirms the subject's growing influence. This occurred both in the real world and in Academia, since a growing number of the new journals focus on, and are clearly a response to the growth of, specialist sub-branches of Economics.

This trend is demonstrated by the American Economic Association's decision to launch a number of new journals. In addition to its major, original journal, the American Economic Review, the Association launched in 2009 four additional journals focusing on Applied Economics, Economic Policy, Macroeconomics and Microeconomics. Other earlier launches include two journals on aspects of Economics: the Journal of Economic Literature (launched 1969) and the Journal of Economic Perspectives (launched 1987). Both of them are influential and enjoy high article-citation impact.

But this is just the tip of a massive iceberg. The ever-expanding number of Economics journals now include, for example: the Journal of Financial Economics, the Journal of Economic Behavior and Organization, the Journal of Finance (published by the AEA since 1974), the Real World Economic Review, the Journal of Economic Modeling, the Journal of Economic Education and many, many others.

Statistics

Another related academic subject also enjoyed a parallel boom in growth: Statistics. Statistics plays a very significant, even dominant, role in the methodology of macroeconomics[5]. Most of the forecasts and 'deductions' of macroeconomics rely on supposedly valid statistically-significant historical correlations. The explosive growth in the study of Economics was matched by a parallel boom in the study of Statistics. The professional body representing statisticians, the **American Statistical Association**, formed in 1839, saw its membership grow from 3,000 in 1939 to a present figure in excess of 19,000.

We Did It! Economists Believe their own Publicity

As the 2000s succeeded the '90s, the Economics profession entered the new century with an exalted and seemingly well-justified confidence in the effectiveness and relevance of the profession and in the superior competence of its practitioners.

With the global economy continuing to grow strongly, economists, led by macroeconomists and government economic advisers, saw their public exposure, prestige and official influence soar. From there it was a short and natural step for them to claim responsibility for the rise in global prosperity. Eager to grab any opportunity to claim credit for positive economic news, economists began to believe that the steady expansion in growth and the steady rise in global stock markets of the Great Moderation, unprecedented though these were, could rightly and deservedly be attributed to their exceptional wisdom and expertise.

This complacent belief in their own excellence was expressed most succinctly in the quotation by Robert Lucas cited at the head of this Chapter. It seemed to macroeconomists perfectly reasonable and justifiable to give themselves a great big public pat on the back. After all, they had solved the central problem of Economics (and the key policy problem facing governments) - generating steady, non-inflationary growth.

As noted, in February, 1999, **Alan Greenspan, Lawrence Summers** and **Robert Rubin** were hailed, in an adulatory cover article in TIME magazine, as 'The Committee to Save the World' for their action to avert market disorder following the collapse of the hedge fund Long Term Capital Management (LTCM) in September, 1998, due to the fund's extreme leverage in a wide variety of flawed derivative positions.

This public applause further encouraged the ready assumption by economists that the methods and practice of Economics had attained a level of explanatory and predictive reliability which thoroughly justified their enhanced public status and prestige. In short, economists everywhere began to believe their own publicity.

Unfortunately this complacent confidence in the expertise of economists was taken up uncritically and enthusiastically by politicians (who were happy to climb on the band-wagon), commentators (who should have known better) and in turn the general public. In the end it was, as ever, the latter - you and me - who were to be the fall-guys when the worst financial crisis since the Great Depression struck in 2008.

Chapter 1, Part 2: Notes

1. According to a report in the Economist, cited by Alan Greenspan in his book 'The Map and the Territory', by 2007 a quarter of all graduates of the California Institute of Technology were entering finance.
2. A comment at the time (in an article by W.L Linden published in January, 1991, in Forbes magazine) gives a flavor of the management/partner attitude. 'Having an in-house economist became for many business people something like having a resident astrologer for the medieval royal court: I don't quite understand what this fellow is saying but there must be something to it.'
3. During this period another practice from the world of investment management became increasingly widespread and was rapidly institutionalized, increasing the media exposure of the financial and economic world: the practice of making, towards the end of each year, public forecasts of various key market and economic indicators for the coming year - the level of stock markets, exchange rates, growth and inflation rates, interest rates etc. Every bank, investment management firm and mutual fund, besides many independent advisory firms, contributed predictions. These were, and still are, widely publicized in league tables of predictive forecasts in the Wall Street Journal, Barron's and other financial sector journals. They further increased the media exposure of Economics and economists (though the chief result has been to demonstrate the lamentable predictive competence of these experts, even for very short-term predictions).
4. The journals cited are all USA-based but similar journals were launched in the major developed economies during the same period: e.g. Economica (UK, 1921), Revue d'Histoire Economique et Sociale (France, 1913), Kyoto Economic Review (Japan, 1926).
5. See Chapter 9 on the fallacies in the use of statistics in Economics.

Chapter 2

∿

THE CRISIS OF 2008

PART 1: ORIGINS AND CAUSES

Global Economy: Outlook - Set Fair

In the first few years after the start of the new millennium in 2000, therefore, the world economy and global markets looked to be in robust health. The mini-panic over possible turmoil arising from the amendment of electronic system dating procedures to accommodate the new millennium proved unjustified and the global economy, which had expanded steadily since the Fed's decisive move to throttle inflation in 1982, nearly doubled in size between 2000 and 2008. World trade grew strongly, from around 51% of global GDP in 2000 to more than 60% of a much larger global GDP in 2008.[1]

The global financial system also seemed robust and healthy. The strong and steady expansion of world trade and the growing strength of the emerging market economies, as they played an increasing role in the global economy, encouraged the world's major commercial banks to extend their global reach with acquisitions of banks and/or the creation of branches in the emerging economies and a growing participation in international financing. In fact everything in the global economic and financial garden looked very rosy.

Cracks in the Edifice

As the global economy continued to grow strongly in the first years of the new century, the US supervisory team, now including the new

Federal Reserve chairman, Ben Bernanke, basked in uncritical and def-erential esteem from the politicians and the media. The comment in October, 2007, by John McCain that 'if Alan Greenspan should die, we should pretend he was still alive', exemplified the obsequious respect accorded to him and the other members of the US Economics team.

However, as the new millennium proceeded, some significant cracks began to appear in the global economic edifice. These indicated that underneath its serene, impressive surface, the foundations on which the Golden Age of Economic Growth rested were becoming more and more unstable. While global stockmarkets were enjoying their 25-year ride on the up escalator, major developments were taking place in the world's financial markets which were to have disastrous consequences and in the end precipitate the 2008 global Crisis. These developments were closely linked and each of them fed and amplified the others.

The major cracks in the edifice were:

- **the explosion in leverage and in risk interdependency** of agents in the global financial system, due in part to

- **the explosive growth of the shadow banking sector and of off-balance-sheet lending**, encouraged by the enthusiastic adoption by the world's larger banks of complex and ill-under-stood statistical risk formulae.

Compounding the massive build-up in risk from these developments were two additional factors:

- **the ill-advised repeal of the U.S Glass-Steagall legislation,** and

- **the negligence of the financial rating agencies** in assigning unrealistic and unjustifiable low-risk ratings to a large range of newly-devised, artificial and high-risk debt securities.

Global Financial System: the $674 trillion Time Bomb

The most dangerous weakness in the global financial system, which was in the end to prove lethal, was fundamental and structural: the enormous and rapid increase in the level of debt and leverage both of private individuals and in the global banking and financial system and, thanks to the use of derivatives, the explosion in interdependency between the world's financial institutions.

- **Debt**

During the period from 1980 to 2007, according to the Federal Reserve, US household debt rose from just under 70% of disposable income to nearly 130%. This figure exceeded by far the earlier highest relative debt level, which had been reached just before the collapse of the US stock market in 1929 and the onset of the Great Depression. Similar figures for unprecedented levels of personal debt were recorded in the UK, Canada, the Netherlands and Australia.

The reasons are well known. The growth in debt sprang from the growing optimism which became widespread during this period: continuously rising real estate prices, encouraging both excessive borrowing by private individuals and indiscriminate and unscrupulous lending on the part of banks, together with widespread 'this time it's different' thinking, notably and not least, on the part of the US Federal Reserve.

- **Bank Leverage and Moore's Law**

At the same time, while private debt was ballooning, the world's banks were expanding enormously. Some of this expansion was attributable to traditional commercial lending and related transactions as the global economy grew and world trade expanded. But a vastly greater proportion of the growth of banks during this period, and in particular the huge increase in the leverage they took on, sprang from a major shift in the focus, balance and volume of their business and this was attributable to developments in computing power.

In the 1980s and '90s developments in communications but even more the exponential growth in 'bang-for-the-buck' computing power and performance, encouraged two dramatic and fundamental changes in the activities of most of the world's commercial and investment banks and in the global financial system. Both of these changes led to the abandonment of experienced professional human judgment in the operations and risk-control systems of banks in favor of the adoption of abstract, untested computer models.

The first of these changes was more regrettable than systemically dangerous.[2] It was the jettisoning of operational credit practices proven over centuries in favor of standardized computer-generated quantitative formulae. In the good old days BC (before computers) banking meant knowing your customers well. Loan decisions were based as much on qualitative, individual judgments of a borrower's credit-worthiness, including his personal character, as on formulaic financial analysis.

This sound process, the basis of the successful practice and conduct of banking for centuries, began to be replaced, about 40 years ago, by an industry-wide move to cut costs through the adoption of standardized formulae for credit decisions, as computing and communications advances encouraged banks to standardize and centralize their credit decision procedures and competition put increasing pressure on them to reduce staff and management costs.

• Rocket Scientists, Rocketing Leverage

But the second consequence of the collapse in the cost of computing power was much more dangerous and was to play a major role in the run-up to the global financial Crisis of 2008. The great increase in computer power spurred the development of a range of elaborate models and formulae which defined and quantified, reliably so it was claimed, the risks of newly-invented, complex derivative contracts in the financial markets, particularly in the debt and bond markets. These statistical models had a common feature: all of them purported to prove that the risks of a wide range of derivative positions and debt securities could be accurately assessed and quantified - they could be regarded as reliably grounded in fact. Consequently the models justified a large and ballooning range of unrestrained credit and risk judgments and a ballooning volume of risky business.

These theoretical constructs led to an explosion, first, in the creation and marketing of investment securities based on these supposedly reliable models and, secondly, in the volume of derivative contracts traded between financial agents. Many, if not most, of these securities would not have seen the light of day before the advent of computers. In the event, market participants were happy to prefer these abstract, theoretical calculations over risk and exposure judgments based on the exercise of experience and prudence, such as had defined the business of banking for centuries.[3]

• The Big Banks: Musical Chairs

'As long as the music is playing, you've got to get up and dance': **Chuck Prince**, CEO, Citibank, July 9th, 2007.

As the over-confidence and euphoria generated by the Golden Age of Growth continued to sprinkle its magic dust on the financial markets the prevailing view among major financial institutions was that, in the words of Chuck Prince of Citibank: 'if the music's still playing we're still dancing'.

Any ambitious financial institution worth its salt set up a trading desk to trade with the bank's money (i.e. the money of the bank's shareholders) as a principal for its own account rather than as an agent acting on behalf of the bank's clients. This lent a powerful additional thrust to the volume of business and the reach of these markets. Most of this expansion in volume was transacted in the various derivative contracts available in the major financial markets (forwards, futures and options in foreign exchange, equities, bonds and commodities) with the major focus on the market for debt.

The largest commercial banks, Citibank, Deutsche Bank, BNP etc., discovered that in the prevailing bubbly financial markets they could make much more money by arranging and packaging issues of debt for borrowers and by trading those instruments than by the tedious, capital-and-staff-intensive and much less profitable traditional business of taking deposits and making loans. Accordingly they turned themselves into investment banks. Many also created off-balance sheet entities to hold these exposures, thereby avoiding or emasculating regulatory and prudential control of their risk exposure. Similarly, the investment banks, like Goldman Sachs, Morgan Stanley and Bear Stearns, downgraded their traditional business of raising money for US industry and focused on morphing into hedge funds, wheeling and dealing for their own account in the financial markets.

By the time of the Crisis the volume of outstanding derivative contracts between financial agents had soared to more than forty times the size of the US economy, ten times the size of the global economy and more than four times the estimated total value of global investment assets.[4] Relying on these flawed risk models the world's commercial and investment banks took on massive leverage.[5]

- ## The Global Debt Supercycle

For a (very) few of the more thoughtful and experienced economic commentators the Crisis of 2008 looked like the culmination of the latest replay of a cycle which regularly recurred in the world economy: the repeated resort to increased debt to solve economic recessions and the need for ever-larger amounts of debt to counteract the effects of each recession. One of the best brief analyses of the so-called Debt Supercycle is given in three research articles by the Montreal-based investment research firm, **BCA Research.**[6]

The $674 trillion Time Bomb

The consequence of this explosion in the size of the unregulated global derivatives market was a corresponding **explosion in risk-interdependency**, enormous in both size and extent, among the world's private-sector banks and financial institutions. At its peak the sum of the liabilities outstanding between the world's private-sector banks and financial institutions amounted to $674 trillion, ten times the size of the global economy, with the soundness of these positions resting overwhelmingly on theoretical, artificial, untested risk formulae.

A House Built on Sand

What this rise in private and public debt and in leverage in the global and US financial systems demonstrated was that the sustained economic growth of the Golden Age and the unprecedented rise in the world's stock markets rested on consumption and investment which sprang not from solid earnings, profits and savings but from the enormous increase in debt and the parallel boom in financial smoke-and-mirrors operations. It was therefore fragile and vulnerable - it was a bubble which could only be sustained if the very favorable monetary conditions which generated it continued indefinitely and, even more crucially, if the mutual confidence and trust which enables banks and financial agents to deal with and lend to each other across the globe remained undiminished.

Chapter 2, Part 1: Notes

1. Source: the World Bank.
2. Although it made much easier the adoption and operation of the flawed standardized credit procedures of the banking and near-banking institutions like Countrywide, specializing in mortgage lending to private borrowers.
3. The essential, and attractive, feature of these models was that they provided apparent proof of the validity and reliability of the risk calculations they modelled. As the Crisis was to demonstrate, the models were profoundly flawed and very dangerous. The uncritical acceptance by bank managements of these risk models led to the replacement of professional experience and judgment, in assessing the overall risk of a bank's exposure to a wide range of assets, by processes based on abstract, formulaic computer programs. These programs turned out to be flawed and, in the end, lethal.

   The really attractive feature of these contracts (from the point of view of a bank's trading business) is that they enable the taking of substantial positions with little or no security or margin. The potential profit from a successful trade is enormously increased by the leverage available in the contract. If you are putting up 1% or 2% of the value of a deal (or even, if you are sufficiently large and your name is good enough, 0%) then you stand to gain 100-200% of your outlay if the acquired security moves, as many markets do, by 1% or 2% in a single day (providing of course you bet the right way).

   In the global f/x market for example, the estimated proportion of market volume attributable to fundamental trade or investment transactions is well below 5%, with the 95% balance being positions taken on the basis of a speculative bet. (George Soros' shorting of Sterling at the time of its ill-judged EMS experience in 1982 is perhaps the best-known and most spectacular and successful example of the kind of trade constituting the vast bulk of f/x trading volume but there were many more (for example the $7.2 billion loss recorded by the French bank Societe Generale as a result of unfortunate trading by one of its employees).)
4. The development of the derivatives market also led to a number of ethically questionable transactions. It was easy to devise derivatives to hide debt or roll it forward to the future. Thus Goldman Sachs devised derivatives to hide the excessive level of Greek public debt in the run up to the Greek application for

membership of the Eurozone. The same accusation was made against Italy. There were many others and many led to later lawsuits against the financial institutions responsible for promoting them. An additional questionable innovation in the use of derivatives came with the disclosure that Goldman Sachs had devised a derivative to bet on the failure of a derivative it had developed to meet the requirements of an existing client. Heads I Win, Tails You Lose! - Goldman were on both sides of the deal.

5.   Details of the extreme extent of leverage in the financial system can easily be found in many books, DVDs etc. and also in The Federal Crisis Commission Report, 2011.

6.   i) More Thoughts on the Debt Supercycle; The Final Inning?, March 3rd, 2009; ii) Debt Supercycle & Public Finances: Where is the Next Crisis?, February 23rd, 2010; and iii) The Financial Crisis of 2007-09: Where Do We Go from Here?, June 15th, 2010.

PART 2: THE CRISIS- EFFECTS AND CONSEQUENCES

'The Federal Reserve is not currently forecasting a recession.' **Ben Bernanke**, Jan 10th, 2008.

'The risk that the economy has entered a substantial downturn appears to have diminished over the past month or so.' **Ben Bernanke**, June 9th, 2008.

'When I was sitting there at the Fed, I would say, "Does anyone know what is going on?"… I couldn't tell what was happening. And the answer was, "Only in part." '. **Alan Greenspan**, interview with **Gillian Tett**, Financial Times, October 26th, 2013.

On September 15th, 2008, **Lehman Brothers**, the US investment bank, filed for Chapter 11 bankruptcy. The filing came after a frantic search for a solution to the bank's inability to fund itself in an increasingly panicky marketplace and after the failure of the US authorities to step in and rescue it. It was this last failure which really unnerved global financial markets. The bank had an enormously overleveraged balance sheet, with extremely dubious assets of $639 billion offsetting debts of $619 billion and shareholders' funds of $22 billion.

Earlier, in March of that year, when **Bear Stearns** had also tottered on the edge of collapse, after a run on its funding sources, the Federal Reserve had arranged a rescue to preserve the stability of the financial markets. Utterly against market expectations, it decided against doing so for Lehman. The Fed's failure to step in as lender-of-last-resort to prevent the collapse of Lehman Brothers, as it had earlier stepped in to rescue Bear Stearns, was devastating. It raised instantly the specter of massive credit contamination and widespread default. It was in fact the straw that broke the back of the world's financial markets.

GLOBAL COLLAPSE

When the Fed refused to bail out Lehman Brothers the smoke-and-mirrors fragility of the US and global debt pyramid became devastatingly apparent. The immediate impact was an instant worldwide freezing of the global financial system, with a collapse in interbank dealings and even the suspension of the basic process of the short-term financing of global trade, as banks worldwide refused to accept on trust the soundness and solvency of their counterparts.

Many books have been published analyzing the Crisis and its origins and the actions taken by officials as the Crisis intensified. The details of how the global financial system was driven, in the course of a single week, to the brink of total collapse, have been well and exhaustively described.[1] The flood of books includes descriptions, explanations and commentaries by professional economists and more useful analyses by respected and authoritative economic journalists (see Chapter 4).

Besides independent comments there have been explanations and commentaries, mostly self-exculpating, by the major authors of the Crisis and their accomplices (**Alan Greenspan, Ben Bernanke**, etc.). There have also been apologetic musings by many of the practicing macroeconomists with public pulpits who failed to foresee the Crisis (**Paul Krugman**).

In addition there have been a number of good 'fly-on-the-wall/you were there' reports (e.g. **Andrew Ross Sorkin's** book **'Too Big to Fail'** and **'Never Let a Serious Crisis go to Waste'** by **Philip Mirowski**) and some excellent TV programs, particularly in the **PBS Frontline** series, **'The Economic Meltdown'**. Two further programs, also available on DVD, **'Money, Power and Wall Street'** and especially **'Inside Job'**, spell out in detail the culpable connections and guilty parties covering, importantly, the bail-out with tax-payer funds of the very Wall Street firms responsible for the Crisis. Narrower in scope but equally watchable is **'The Big Short'**, based on the book with the same title by **Michael Lewis**. Together these give a clear, simple and comprehensive analysis of the structural origins of the Crisis, of its rapid metastasis through the world's financial system and of the official responses and actions to prevent it permanently destabilizing the global economy. These descriptions are non-technical and thorough and those interested in the details will have no difficulty in finding them from these and a wide selection of other sources.

THE EFFECTS OF THE CRISIS

The consequences of the Crisis for the global economy, both immediate and longer-term, were catastrophic. They have been comprehensively described in many works (very well, again, in the **PBS Frontline** series). The major disastrous effects of the Crisis are summarized below.

The Effects of the Crisis: Immediate

The immediate consequences of the Crisis were:

- the instant freezing of the global banking and financial system,

- a resulting collapse in world trade,

- rapid recessions in the developed economies,

- a precipitous collapse in the world's stock markets and, in short order,

- an explosive increase in global unemployment.

The annual rate of global GDP growth fell from +4% at the start of 2007 to -4.5% in the third quarter of 2008 as the Crisis struck. Global trade growth collapsed from +6.5% to -18.0% over the same period. The Baltic Dry Index, the index of the global demand for cargo ships and therefore a good indicator of the strength of world trade, fell by more than 90% in 2008. Unemployment in the USA which had been 5% in December, 2007, shot up to 9.5% in June, 2009, and to 10% in October of that year. Similar collapses in employment were recorded in the other developed economies. Globally, according to a September, 2010, report by the IMF, the Crisis caused unemployment to jump by 30 million.

The above statistics demonstrate the rapid and extensive global devastation wreaked by the Crisis. This was not simply some cyclical deterioration in economic or financial statistics; the Crisis did disastrous damage to the lives and well-being of victims numbering, immediately, many tens of millions and, in due course, hundreds of millions throughout the world.

As an immediate step to counter and offset the global financial emergency, massive injections of liquidity into the US financial system were achieved through purchases by the Federal Reserve in the US Treasury bond market. Short-term interest rates were reduced to 1%, and later to zero. Similar liquidity programs were adopted by other central banks in the hope that this strategy would be effective in generating a return to the former levels of positive economic growth.

The Effects of the Crisis: Persistent

The disastrous effects of the Crisis were not only short-term; they continue to weigh on much of the global economy. The longer-term economic consequences of the Crisis - even now, more than ten years after the event - are still with us.

They include:

- pervasive stagnant or below-historical-trend economic growth,

- continued high real unemployment and underemployment in many of the major economies,

- an explosion in debt, both sovereign and private, in most of the developed economies,

- deflation with the risk of a descent into debt deflation,

- exceptionally low and in some cases negative real interest rates with a severe depressive effect on savings, investment and consumption and continued severe misallocation of investment,

- policy paralysis on the part of central banks and finance ministries,

- financial markets which have lost touch with the real world and have become increasingly artificial,

- pervasive uncertainty and pessimism.

Stagnation

The condition of negligible or no economic growth in a market economy was branded as 'secular stagnation' by **Larry Summers** in a February, 2016, article in Foreign Affairs. A more thorough description and analysis of the origins of the stagnant growth still afflicting many developed countries is presented by **Richard Koo**, then chief economist of the Nomura Research Institute, in his 2009 book **'The Holy Grail of Macroeconomics: Lessons from Japan's Great Recession'**. Koo analyzes the economic weakness prevailing in much of the world as a 'balance sheet recession' resulting from the policy inflexibility imposed by excess debt.[2]

Debt: Not Waving but Drowning

The pre-Crisis explosion in private debt to well above the level of household income had its malign counterpart after the Crisis struck and as a policy response to it, in the form of a massive increase in the level of government debt, as the governments of the developed economies stepped in to prevent wholesale catastrophe. The bankruptcy of Lehman Brothers on September 15th, 2008, triggered an instantaneous collapse in liquidity in the world's financial and money markets. Overnight even the largest global banks and financial intermediaries were unable to fund their operations in the marketplace.

The global financial system was at risk of terminal breakdown. Faced with this threat the Federal Reserve and other G7 central banks took action to backstop their banking systems, providing loans, arranging the disposal or merger of critically weak institutions to other safer hands and fulfilling their textbook role as lenders of last resort in a systemic liquidity crisis.

The consequence has been that the extreme levels of private debt in the larger developed economies before the Crisis are now matched by stratospheric, unprecedented levels of government debt. In most developed economies government debt as a proportion of the size of the economy has soared, with the average ratio of debt to GDP surging from 70% in 2007 to 110% in 2012 and to more than 130% in 2017.[3] This growth shows no signs of stopping. Furthermore, these increases have come on top of still record levels of private debt. So far from falling, private debt remains above its level at the onset of the Crisis. The consequence is that total global debt is now, at $270 trillion, more than three times global GDP.[4]

A precondition of any stable resolution of the massive debt problem now overhanging the developed economies is a return to sustained and significant positive growth. Alas, this remains, more than ten years after the Crisis, a distant prospect.

Policy Straightjacket

Yet the most toxic consequence of the massive increase in government debt in the developed economies may be the severe restrictions it has placed on the room for maneuver in the management of their economies and in particular in the event of future financial crises. If your debt is equal to the size of your economy then even a small rise in interest rates above your growth rate will further increase your debt burden. It is concern on this point which has lain behind the clear hesitation of the Federal Reserve in the USA and the ECB in Europe to raise interest rates too fast and too far.

Investment Misallocation: Zombie Companies, Zombie Economies

Another serious consequence of the debt problem is that the ultra-low interest rates which have been one of the results of the Crisis encourage persistent investment misallocation. In remarks introducing a paper at a recent conference, **Claudio Borio**, of the Bank for International Settlements, drew attention to the malign growth in the numbers of 'zombie' companies[5]. A 'zombie' company is defined as a company at least 10 years old, with low growth prospects, whose profits are insufficient to cover debt interest payments. According to the OECD, the share of 'zombie' companies in developed economies has risen to 10%. A consequence of this increase is a corresponding fall in productivity. With enough zombie companies, you have an increasingly zombie economy.

QUANTITATIVE EASING

The initial response to the Crisis, in the USA and elsewhere, was a massive injection of liquidity into the financial system. In the USA this was achieved through purchases by the Federal Reserve in the US Treasury bond market and the slashing of short-term interest rates; similar liquidity programs were adopted by other central banks. The hope was that this strategy would be effective not just in stemming the Crisis but also in ensuring a return to former levels of positive economic growth.

In the event the liquidity central banks stumped up to avert the collapse of the global financial system turned out to be just a small first downpayment on what became hugely larger programs of monetary support to their economies. The programs came to be called Quantitative Easing (QE), as persistent fear and uncertainty replaced confidence and economic growth slumped and then stagnated.

The Failure of QE

These programs have now essentially been maintained for more than ten years. The initial expectation was that this enormous and unprecedented monetary stimulus would not only stop the Crisis in its tracks and prevent a second Great Depression but also, in accordance with the predictions of the dominant macroeconomic model followed by the world's central banks, generate a rapid recovery, returning the global economy to the strong growth it had long enjoyed before 2008. So far the programs have failed to generate a durable return to sustained growth. After more than 10 years of sustained and massive monetary stimulus, growth remains significantly below its long term trend in the developed economies and is only now climbing weakly into positive territory.

As noted, if a country's debt load exceeds the size of its economy the rate of interest it pays to roll over its debt must be lower than its growth rate or the debt will continue to grow. With growth rates in the developed economies at 2% or lower any significant rise in interest rates from their present ultra-low levels (or even a meaningful cessation or tapering of the QE programs) would be very dangerous.

Since a return to sustained positive growth (the precondition of any stable resolution of their problem) remains a distant prospect, many countries, including, within the straight-jacket of the Eurozone, Italy, Greece and Portugal, with France on the brink, have now crossed the event-horizon of debt default. (Japan, with government debt at more than 200% of GDP, has so far been given a pass by the markets. The reasons for this are first that most of its debt is held by Japanese households and secondly that the country's external assets very substantially exceed its liabilities.) Unlike the Eurozone members, the UK benefits from the flexibility of having its own currency. For the time being, however, global investors have suspended their critical faculties, closed their eyes and minds and accepted on blind faith the wishful, Micawberish assurances from Eurozone central bankers that it will all work out OK in the end.

Another consequence of the QE monetary stimulus programs has been that the balance sheets of the major central banks have exploded. From around US$ 850 billion before the Crisis the balance sheet of the US Federal Reserve now stands at more than US$ 6 trillion. The ECB was slower to adopt QE but its balance sheet footings have more than quadrupled from around Euros 1.5 trillion before the Crisis to in excess of Euros 6.5 trillion. Today, more than ten years after the Crisis, the balance sheets of the central banks of the major developed economies (the US Federal Reserve, the European Central Bank, the Bank of Japan, the Bank of England) stand at an aggregate figure of more than US$15 trillion.

Yet interest rates remain at record low levels. This combination, of crisis-induced zero and near-zero interest rates and balance sheets at unprecedented sky-high levels, leaves the central banks essentially impotent in the face of future economic events. They have lost any ability to fulfil their primary role in controlling and regulating monetary policy. The present hesitant moves and statements of the US Federal Reserve are an indication of how uncomfortable they find this persistent impotence.

Chapter 2, Part 2: Notes

1. **'The Two Trillion Dollar Meltdown'**, by **Charles Morrison,** one of the few to predict the Crisis, written shortly after it, gives a detailed record of the meltdown.
2. There is however a persuasive alternative analysis and interpretation of the depressive economic forces now impacting the developed economies. This analysis sees the major impulse for the persistent slowdown in growth as the possible ending, after 250 years, of the central social and economic process triggered by the Industrial Revolution: the seemingly natural and automatic causal link between economic growth and stronger well-paid employment. According to this analysis the explosive growth and spread, globally, of the automated production of goods services, enhanced by Artificial Intelligence, presages the end of this growth/employment nexus.
3. Source: OECD figures for G7 economies.
4. See also: McKinsey Global Institute: Debt and (Not Much) Deleveraging. February, 2015.
5. 'Weak productivity: the role of financial factors and policies', January 10-11th, 2018, presented at a recent BIS-IMF-OECD conference in Paris.

Chapter 3

WHOSE FAULT WAS IT?
WHO SAW IT COMING?

For the purposes of this book the details of the disastrous effects of the Crisis are relatively unimportant and have been well described in many books. What *is* important is the reason for the actions and inaction which led to the Crisis and the failure of the economic theories which they were based on.

Many factors contributed to the 2008 Crisis. Some of them may reasonably be considered as external factors resulting from the long-wave, secular and structural processes of global growth, global demographics and technological progress and thus beyond the control of regulators (although, particularly as regards the consequences of the explosion in computing power and its effect in the credit markets, the growing impact of some of these factors was clearly discernible and should have been foreseen).

But the important factors fell fully within the purview and control of the US financial authorities - the Federal Reserve and the US Treasury. The actions and policy decisions in the period leading up to the Crisis were taken chiefly by the US Federal Reserve, in its capacity as supervisor of the US economy and regulator of the US banking system, the epicenter of the Crisis.

PART 1: DERELICTION OF DUTY: THE FAILURE OF THE FED

There were two immediate causes of the Federal Reserve's failure to foresee and prevent the Crisis:

- **the failure of the Federal Reserve to regulate and control the explosive growth of credit in the US economy,** and
- **the repeal in 1999 of the long-standing Glass-Steagall Act.**

Underlying these was a third error which was predominant and lethal:

- **the comprehensive failure of the principal economic model used by the Fed in mapping and managing the US economy.**

Behind the regulatory and economic policies followed by the Fed in the years running up to the Crisis lay the Fed's model of the US economy. It was the unwavering confidence of the Fed and of its Chairman, Alan Greenspan, in the validity and reliability of its preferred macro-economic model which was the key origin of the policy failures which led to the Crisis. It is this disastrous professional failure and the reasons for it which are the subject of this book.

The Guilty Parties

The decisive role in this gross failure of fiduciary responsibility was played by three individuals: **Alan Greenspan, Lawrence Summers** and **Ben Bernanke,** Greenspan's successor as Chairman of the Federal Reserve, with **Robert Rubin,** then chairman of Goldman Sachs, as a fourth accomplice.

- **Alan Greenspan,** had been appointed Chairman of the Federal Reserve in August, 1987, after serving as Chair of President Gerald Ford's Council of Economic Advisers and a decade pursuing a private consulting career. He was Chairman of the Federal Reserve until January, 2006.[1]

- **Lawrence Summers**, after a stint as Chief Economist of the World Bank, served as Deputy Treasury Secretary to Robert Rubin from 1995-1999 and then succeeded Rubin in July, 1999, as Treasury Secretary under President Clinton, serving until 2001.

- **Ben Bernanke** succeeded Greenspan as Fed chairman in February, 2006, holding the position through the Crisis and retiring in February, 2014.

- **Robert Rubin**, formerly co-chairman of the investment bank Goldman Sachs, was appointed Economics Adviser to President Clinton in January, 1993 and then Treasury Secretary from 1995-1999.

It was these four officials who presided over the explosion in credit in the run-up to the Crisis and who oversaw, and even encouraged, in the years before the Crisis, the dismantling of the key prudential regulations and laws which prevented banks from taking on excessive leverage and excessive risk exposure.

Dereliction of Duty 1: Uncontrolled Credit

'Banks are largely sophisticated financial institutions that would appear to be eminently capable of protecting themselves from fraud and counterparty insolvencies.' **Lawrence Summers**, testimony to Congress, 1998.

'There is growing recognition that the dispersion of credit risk by banks to a broader and more diverse set of investors....has helped make the banking and overall financial system more resilient.' **IMF**, Global Stability Report, April, 2006.

'With respect to their safety, derivatives, for the most part, are traded among very sophisticated financial institutions and individuals who have considerable incentive to understand them and to use them properly.' **Ben Bernanke**, Nov 15th, 2005.

'I made a mistake in presuming that the self-interest of organizations, specifically banks and others were such that they were best capable of protecting their own shareholders and their equity in the firms.' **Alan Greenspan**, remarks to the House Committee on Oversight and Government Reform, October 23rd, 2008.

First and foremost in the derelictions of duty by the Federal Reserve which led to the Crisis was its failure to fulfil its primary responsibility as regulator of the US financial system by controlling the growth of credit. By failing to control the explosive growth in credit in the financial system, whether it took the form of direct loans or off-balance sheet lending by the banking system or through increasing derivative exposure, the Fed presided in the years before the Crisis over a massive increase in liquidity in the US economy. This policy failure was replicated in the other developed economies.

Some have seen the origin of the explosion in credit in a global savings glut, as the volume of global money seeking investment outweighed the demand for finance. This seems simply an evasive answer. If there was an excess of footloose savings looking for a useful home in the global economy that in no way excuses the failure of the US authorities to prevent it destabilizing the US financial system.

The back-and-forth of finger-pointing and accusation and denial continues to this day but the central regulatory failure was one which has nothing to do with competitive economic theories. It goes back to the crucial and long-established overriding duty of central banks: to maintain stability in the financial system. This responsibility is the rationale of the supreme guiding principle of central banking (see below: The Golden Rule).

The explosive and dangerous growth in credit went hand-in-hand with an equally dangerous failure on the part of the authorities responsible for regulating and controlling the banking system: their uncritical complacency as to the growing level of risk in the system. It was not just banks and financial executives on Wall Street who were happy to delude themselves that their businesses were not becoming riskier and riskier.

The very officials in the Fed and the Treasury, whose responsibility it was to prevent the growth of undue levels of risk in the US financial system, accepted uncritically and without demur the arguments presented by the same banks that all was well and that any problems would be self-adjusting and therefore did not present any serious risk to the entire system. They were happy, in fact, to go along with the belief that 'this time is different'.

'This Time is Different'

There was absolutely nothing unusual or new in the Crisis of 2008. Throughout history financial crises and panics have occurred with reliable frequency in all of the developed economies. A recent essay in The Economist records financial crises in the USA in 1792, 1825, 1837, 1857, 1873, 1907, 1929, etc.[2] The creation of the Federal Reserve in 1913 to assume the role of lender-of-last-resort to the fragmented and unregulated US banking system was an outcome of, and a response to, the devastation wreaked by the 1907 crash.

The distinguishing feature of these crises, and of every financial crisis from the tulip mania in the Netherlands in 1692 to the South Sea Bubble in the UK in 1720 and since, is that without exception they arose from excessive speculation enabled by uncontrolled credit. The Crisis of 2008 was no exception. It was simply the latest, though by far the most globally devastating, in the long series of crises which have regularly punctuated the history of human financial behavior.

The Golden Rule: Take Away the Punchbowl Before the Party Gets Out-of-Hand!

The essential role and responsibility of central banks is to supervise and control the monetary systems in their economies, managing the price and availability of credit. Their task is to ensure stability through fluctuating economic conditions and business cycles, preventing depressions by easing credit at the bottom of the cycle and preventing inflationary bubbles by restricting it at the cycle top.

There is a golden rule which central banks must follow in managing the availability of credit in their economy and it requires the strictest observance. The importance of this prudential rule cannot be overstated; it has always been and remains the first and greatest commandment in the central bank operational rule book.

The essential principle in question dates back to the English commentator on banking and the financial markets in the 19th century, **Walter Bagehot**, and was set out in his book '**Lombard Street**'. It has long been accepted as the key principle guiding central bank policy in the regulation of a country's financial markets. It was endorsed in a speech in October, 1955, by **William McChesney Martin**, the then Chairman of the Federal Reserve, specifically advocating 'precautionary [*Government*] action 'to prevent inflationary excesses".[3]

As McChesney Martin succinctly put it: 'The Government's responsibility (*i.e., in the US, by delegation, the responsibility of the Federal Reserve, the US Government's agent in the financial markets*) is to 'take away the punch bowl before the party gets out-of-hand'; that is to say, to control the availability of credit to prevent financial bubbles which might destabilize the economic system. The sustained relaxation of restrictions on credit in its many forms during the period leading up to the Crisis of 2008 directly contravened this fundamental and essential rule.

There was no secret, in the bubbles of 1873, 1913, 1955 or in 2008, as to the measures necessary to enable effective control of the levels of liquidity and credit in the economy. Direct credit creation by the banking system could be limited by imposing appropriate capital and reserve requirements on banks. Excessive expansion in indirect credit (via off-balance-sheet operations and other shadow banking maneuvers, margin lending) could be controlled by appropriately stiff regulations and by margin requirements.)

Throughout history, from John Law's Mississippi bubble of the 1720s in France and the contemporary South Sea Bubble in the UK, through the 19th century railway bubble and the market crash of 1929 and the more recent dot.com bubble of 2000 and the 2008 Crisis, uncontrolled credit has been at the heart of all major financial crashes.[4]

Dereliction of Duty 2: Who Needs Regulations?

The crucial impetus encouraging the dangerous growth of interdependency and risk in the US, and by extension in the global, financial system came from the failure of the Federal Reserve and the US Treasury to regulate and limit it. In the years before 2008 the Fed persistently failed to take the necessary action to prevent the flood of excess credit washing into the economy. The consequence was that the system duly crashed.

In fact, so far from taking steps to regulate and limit the explosion in credit in the economy and control the build-up of risk as the US economy roared ahead and both debt and risk exploded, the Fed was happy to relax steadily the regulations controlling the US banking and financial system. Many of these prudential regulations had been adopted specifically to prevent the re-emergence of the structural flaws in the financial system which had led to the excesses which triggered the Great Depression. The laws and regulations adopted after the Great Depression were designed specifically to help the Fed and the

US Treasury achieve their primary and overriding policy objective of financial stability.

Together, Greenspan (and later Bernanke) at the Federal Reserve and Lawrence Summers at the US Treasury had, on the contrary, encouraged for several years the successive dismantling of these measures. They took steps to steadily relax and ultimately repeal the regulations controlling and limiting the activities of the banks and other agents in the US financial system, including the repeal of the single most important regulation limiting the activities of the banking system in the financial investment market, the Glass-Steagall Act.

In 1998, Greenspan, then Chairman of the Fed, had fought to prevent any regulation of the derivatives market. He, Lawrence Summers and Robert Rubin strongly resisted the proposal by **Brooksley Born** that the Commodities Futures Trading Commission be given authority to supervise and control the growing market in credit derivatives, the financial contracts which played a leading role in the Crisis of 2008. In their view regulation of derivatives was unnecessary.

In December, 2000, with the strong encouragement of the Fed, Congress passed the Commodity Modernization Act. This Act suspended any regulation of over-the-counter derivative transactions between 'sophisticated parties' and opened the door to the explosion in uncontrolled derivative securitization which was a major cause of the Crisis. As these controls were successively lifted in the '90s and in the wake of the market crash of 2000, banks and investment banks were free to take on greater and greater leverage, both through direct borrowing and, even more, through rocketing exposure to derivative contracts with other financial agents.

All along, the argument which Greenspan and his regulatory colleagues presented against any strengthening of regulatory oversight was that banks were perfectly competent to exercise prudent self-regulation of their positions and exposure. The quotations at the head of this section fairly express the complacent belief on the part of Greenspan, Bernanke and Summers that there was nothing to worry about. Other market officials echoed this view. In a paper issued in 2007, just before the Crisis, when the total value of derivative exposure rose above $600 trillion, **William Dudley**, Head of the Markets Group at the New York Federal Reserve, and **Glenn Hubbard**, former Chairman of the Council of Economic Advisers to President G. W. Bush, affirmed their confidence in the safety of the system.

The seeds of this relaxation had been sown in 1980, when Jimmy Carter passed an Act phasing out many restrictions on banks' operations, and were compounded in 1982 by Ronald Reagan's de-regulation Acts, but it was in 1999, during Bill Clinton's presidency, that Lawrence Summers and Robert Rubin supported and engineered the repeal of the Glass-Steagall Act.

The Repeal of Glass-Steagall

The Glass-Steagall Act was the long-standing keystone legislation which limited and controlled the activities of the banking sector. The Act had been passed into law in 1933 in the aftermath of the Great Depression. Its purpose was to distinguish clearly between, and to separate by law and thereby enable the control of, the two activities of commercial and investment banking - to prevent commercial banks from acting as investment banks, and vice versa. It had been passed by the then Congress as a direct reaction to the failure of 5,000 banks following the Stock Market crash of 1929 and the Great Depression, caused in large part by the lack of restrictions on the scope of bank activities.

Ben Bernanke has argued, in his memoir of the Crisis (**'The Courage to Act'**) that Glass-Steagall was irrelevant and would not have prevented many of the innovative quasi-banking activities which were at the heart of the explosive growth in investment banking business by the commercial banks and in their resulting interconnectedness and interdependency. This overlooks or ignores two facts: first, that most of the dangerous increase in credit and interdependency risk occurred after the repeal of the Act in 1999 and, secondly, that the repeal of the Act was an important public stamp of approval from the authorities for the uncontrolled credit-bubble free-for-all which gathered strength during the years leading up to the Crisis.

The fact is that the repeal of the Act amounted to clear public confirmation that the Fed, too, believed that 'this time is different', that innovations in the credit markets had made the Act irrelevant and, above all, that there was no cause for concern.

Dereliction of Duty 3: the Rating Agencies

An important additional stimulus propelling the explosive growth of the debt and derivatives markets came from the major credit-rating agencies **Moody's, Standard & Poor's** and **Fitch**. The business (and the important fiduciary role) of these agencies was to provide independent assessments of the risk of the securities issued by banks and investment banks, in the form of credit ratings.

In practice, the agencies, who were contracted to give public ratings of the risk of these debt securities, were happy to oblige their bank clients by rubber-stamping the risk assessments which emerged from the banks' risk models. Since the agencies were paid by the banking institutions which were creating and marketing the securities being rated they had a major and fundamental conflict-of-interest. As became evident after the Crisis, the risk ratings granted by the agencies to a vast number of the new credit and debt products were wildly unrealistic and in due course they paid a heavy price for their professional delinquency in the form of massive fines.

At the time however this easy-going regime of specious, wildly-optimistic and irresponsible ratings encouraged the managements of commercial and investment banks to delude themselves that they were successfully controlling the levels of risk they were taking on. The ratings also provided a large boost to the expanding market for these risks, enabling originating banks to offload tranches of these risks to other third parties and institutions.

With the apparently independent and favorable risk-validation provided by the agencies, these models were seen as justifying the taking of very large leveraged positions in various markets. The managers of the world's banks and investment banks were delighted to adopt these arguments since they opened the door to massively greater leverage and of course to greater profits and fatter bonuses.

Lessons Ignored

In fact the Fed had had ample prior warning, not once but twice, of the disastrous consequences of placing uncritical trust in the use of derivatives. Both the events in question were dangerous enough to compel the Fed to step in to prevent systemic contagion. Moreover these warnings were not in the far distant past and therefore outside the experience of the incumbent Fed management: both of them happened on **Alan Greenspan**'s watch as Chairman of the Fed and he most of all should have taken on board and heeded the lesson of the potential for systemic contamination and collapse which uncontrolled credit and the use of derivatives could cause.

i)   The Stock-Market Crash of October, 1987

Greenspan's baptism of fire came on Black Monday, October 19th, 1987, soon after he was appointed Chairman of the Federal Reserve, when the US stock market unexpectedly crashed. On that single day the Dow Jones Industrial Average lost more than 500 points. This represented 22.6% of its capitalization at the time, though the fall did come after a rise of more than 44% in the preceding seven months and in the event the Dow finished that year with an overall gain.

The crash was triggered by sudden alarm on the part of market participants as to the validity and security of portfolio insurance contracts. These were a form of derivative purporting to give protection against falls in the value of stock prices. Interestingly, the protection they claimed to give was very similar to the default protection notionally provided by the Credit Default Swaps derivatives which precipitated the 2008 Crisis.

The event should have been a key lesson for Greenspan in the unreliability of formulaic models and the tendency of market participants to take behavior based on them to systemically dangerous extremes.

ii) The Failure of Long Term Capital Management, September, 1998

In September, 1998, the much-vaunted hedge fund, Long Term Capital Management (LTCM), with two Nobel Prize economists and a raft of experienced market professionals and gurus on its board, blew up, brought down by bets on a wide range of diverse and supposedly uncorrelated derivative positions. The fund's balance sheet was leveraged to 40 times its share capital at the date of its collapse. LTCM needed a US$4 billion bailout. In a precursor to its enormously greater bail-out of the financial system after the 2008 Crisis, the US Federal Reserve, under Alan Greenspan, stepped in to forestall any collateral systemic damage to the US financial system.

Yet the key lesson of the LTCM collapse - the crucial importance of the Fed's responsibility to ensure the stability of the financial markets by supervising and controlling the operations of the entire system of credit creation and the operations of banking agents of all kinds - was, in the years leading up to the 2008 Crisis, utterly ignored.

Professional Complacency: Greenspan, Summers and Bernanke

Underlying these professional errors and failures was a delusional complacency on the part of those in charge of the main institutions in the drama, particularly Greenspan, Summers and Bernanke, as to the reliable validity of large-scale economic theories, as to their own competence and expertise and as to the competence and expertise of the institutions they led. This complacency sprang directly from the apparent great success of the Economics profession in generating the Golden Age of growth in the 1980s and '90s. As noted in Chapter 2, this confidence was, regrettably, shared almost universally by legislators and accepted in turn by the general public.

Throughout the years in the run-up to the Crisis Alan Greenspan's policy for the management of the US economy and the credit markets was essentially 'hands-off' - a non-interference approach based on his strong belief in the self-regulating tendency of developed economies to revert naturally to equilibrium and in the supposedly reliable self-interest of agents (i.e. the banks and their managements) in an unregulated, free-market financial system. (In a sense Greenspan's faith in the self-interest of the managements of the major banks was in fact borne out by their behavior; the problem was that the self whose interest they were advancing was their personal self-interest, not the wider public interest of their banks' customers and stability.)

In September, 2007, after his retirement from the chairmanship of the Federal Reserve in 2006, Greenspan did utter a public warning about the housing bubble but this was a very late reversal of his long-held position on the issue.

Earlier, in June, 2007, **Ben Bernanke**, who had taken over the chairmanship of the Federal Reserve in February, 2006, had stated that 'troubles in the sub-prime sector [of the mortgage finance market] seem unlikely to seriously spill over to the broader economy or the financial system.' In fact Bernanke was quite happy to maintain the complacent, 'steady-as-she-goes', laissez-aller, non-interventionist policy of his predecessor.[5,6]

These were the public policy actions and pronouncements of the two chairmen of the Federal Reserve in the run-up to the Crisis. The important question is: what was the professional economic basis for this complacency?

The Mindset of Alan Greenspan

In essence Greenspan's complacent view rested on his deep-seated belief in two of the key assumptions underlying the neo-classical macro-economic model which he, and the Fed, believed in:

- **economic agents could always be relied on to act in their own best interests,** and

- **unstable economic conditions would return naturally to stable equilibrium.**

There was a third article of faith: Greenspan's equally deep-seated belief in the fundamental validity and virtue of free markets and his distrust of regulation. Some part of his free-market, 'no regulation' credo seems to be attributable to his long-standing friendship with the author **Ayn Rand** and his belief in her so-called Objectivist 'philosophy'.[7]

Bubble Psychology: 'We just can't help it'

Some recent commentators, seeking to understand the reason for the seemingly unavoidable string of crises which have regularly beset the business world, have turned to human nature as the explanation of the phenomenon. In his outstanding and comprehensive record of the 2008 Crisis, **Martin Wolf**, as well as making clear the causal link between financial crises and uncontrolled credit, concludes that financial crises are endemic in developed economic systems. Similarly, **Alan Greenspan** has come to the belief that speculative bubbles are an inescapable feature of human behavior.

However, in a body of work from the 1960s onwards, **Hyman Minsky** developed the thesis that economies, if allowed to develop without prudential control, tended to move naturally from stability to instability, as stability encouraged growing complacency, increased risk-taking and, in the end, speculative excess, leading to a financial crisis. He pointed out the crucial failure of the dominant economic models, (including DSGE, the **Dynamic Stochastic General Equilibrium** model), in ignoring the financial sector and financial flows in their modelling. For Minsky there is an undeniable link between the financial markets and the real economy which is crucial to understanding financial crises. The dominant macroeconomic orthodoxy did not then, and does not even now, incorporate credit and financial flows as factors in its economic modelling.

Until the 2008 Crisis vindicated his thinking Minsky's work was for long systematically ignored, not only in Academia but in the central banks and finance ministries responsible for economic policy. **Ben Bernanke** in his book '**Essays on the Great Depression**', brushed aside Minsky's work on the inherent tendency of economies towards instability with a disparaging comment on its failure to assume rational economic behavior.

PART 2: THE CONGRESSIONAL FINANCIAL
CRISIS INQUIRY COMMISSION

'On the other hand, we cannot say the same thing about deregulations, the bailout and the protection of the culprits on Wall Street. We believe that these actions sprang, in fact, from a concerted effort by a group of the top investment banks and their lobbyists in Washington.' **Federal Commission on the Crisis, 2011**.

In May, 2009, the US Congress created the Financial Crisis Inquiry Commission to investigate the causes of the 2008 crisis. The Commission reported in January, 2011. The chief conclusions of the Commission were, among a list of nine items, that:

- **the Crisis was avoidable and should have been foreseen,** and

- **the primary cause of the Crisis was widespread failure in financial regulation and supervision.**

In particular the Report commented, damningly, that:

'More than 30 years of deregulation and reliance on self-regulation by financial institutions, championed by former Federal Reserve chairman Alan Greenspan and others, supported by successive administrations and Congresses, and actively pushed by the powerful financial industry at every turn, had stripped away key safeguards, which could have helped avoid catastrophe.'

The conclusion of the Commission was that 'This crisis was avoidable—the result of human actions, inactions, and misjudgments. Warnings were ignored. The greatest tragedy would be to accept the refrain that no one could have seen this coming and thus nothing could have been done. If we accept this notion, it will happen again.'[8]

〜〜

PART 3: THE REAL CULPRIT: A FAILED ECONOMIC MODEL

'In 2008 all of our models failed - all, across the board.' **Alan Greenspan**, former Chairman, Federal Reserve Bank of the USA, on CNBC, October 7th, 2011.

The immediate cause of the Crisis of 2008 was the utter failure of the US regulatory authorities, the Fed and the US Treasury, to fulfil their primary governance duty - the preservation of the soundness and stability of the US financial system - by controlling and regulating credit.

But there was one crucial failure which underlay these: the flawed macroeconomic model used by the Federal Reserve to analyze and manage the US economy. While the repeal of Glass-Steagall was a significant contributing factor in the failure of the Fed to control and prevent the credit bubble, a much more important reason for the Fed's failure was the institution's uncritical faith in its favorite macroeconomic model. As eventually admitted by **Alan Greenspan** some while after the Crisis struck, the Fed's economic model of the US economy failed and failed completely and comprehensively.

The Fed had for long followed, and had uncritically accepted as economic orthodoxy, the so-called Dynamic Stochastic General Equilibrium model of the US economy. The core tenet of this model is a belief in the inherent tendency of complex economies to return naturally to equilibrium from any imbalance, if left unregulated. The origins of this belief and the reasons for its dominant influence are described at greater length in Chapter 7.

The consequences of this misplaced theoretical faith were catastrophic. Even now, more than ten years after the bankruptcy of Lehman Brothers triggered the Crisis, global growth remains weak, with a wide gap between very weak growth in the developed economies and the somewhat stronger growth in the developing economies. The volume of global trade is little changed from its level in 2008; the Baltic Index only recently climbed back to a level less than half its average value in the years leading up to the Crisis.

Global debt (both private and sovereign) stands at unprecedented, nose-bleed levels; real interest rates are at previously unimagined zero or even negative levels; the world's commercial banks are still trying to recover their health. Deflation, with its lethal impact on the levels of real debt, remains a lingering problem. All this in spite of monetary expansion on a colossal scale. Yet, unbelievably, the prevailing economic model used by the Fed and the US Treasury entirely ignores the role of finance and credit in the economy.

<p style="text-align:center">~~~</p>

PART 4: WE DIDN'T DO IT!

The aftermath of the Crisis saw the publication of accounts of it by two of its main architects: **Alan Greenspan's 'The Map and the Territory'** and **Ben Bernanke's 'The Courage to Act'**.

From these self-serving accounts and from their public statements since the Crisis it is clear that the main perpetrators do not really regard themselves as responsible and culpable to any significant degree for the worst financial Crisis since the Great Depression. Neither of the authors admits any responsibility for the Crisis. The Crisis was not their fault. They didn't do it!

Greenspan's book has the subtitle: **'A Master Class in the Alchemy of Economic Decision-Making'**. He reiterates his commitment to free markets and to the belief that markets are essentially self-regulating. Other tenets in Greenspan's economic world-view are that financial bubbles are a function of human nature and basically inevitable, that forecasting is a 'necessity' of human nature and, most importantly and regrettably, that statistical regression analysis is a reliably valid basis for successful economic forecasting.

Greenspan, it is true, had the grace to admit, in testimony to Congress in October, 2008, that the whole intellectual edifice [of free markets and low regulation] had collapsed. He had, he said, 'made a mistake in presuming that the self-interest of organizations, including banks, was such that they were best capable of protecting their own shareholders'. He was, he said, shocked. He was, and has remained, the only guilty party to admit some responsibility for the worst economic crisis since the Great Depression.

Ben Bernanke succeeded Alan Greenspan as Chairman of the Federal Reserve in 2006. Notably, he was responsible, in the years before the Crisis and in early 2008, for a series of complacent comments on the sound health of the US economy. In particular he readily attributed its sustained economic growth during the so-called Great Moderation not to luck but in large part to the Federal Reserve's enhanced expertise and the wisdom and competence of the Economics profession.

Hamlet without the Prince

The really remarkable feature of both books is that there is almost no discussion whatever (in Greenspan's book a short sentence, in Bernanke's nothing) of the central role played by the Fed's preferred macroeconomic model in their utter failure to anticipate the Crisis. This model, the so-called **Dynamic Stochastic General Equilibrium** model (DSGE), played the decisive part in the Fed's comprehensive failure to foresee the Crisis and to take steps to prevent it. DSGE and macroeconomics do not even appear in the books' indexes.

PART 5: WHO SAW IT COMING?
THE CASSANDRAS AND WISE VIRGINS

'Few, if any, people anticipated the sort of meltdown that we are seeing in the credit markets at present.' **Robert Rubin**, at the Brookings Institution in Washington, March 14th, 2008.

The truth is, as the Federal Commission on the Crisis concluded, that the Crisis occurred in spite of the overwhelming and growing evidence, in full, plain view, of the unrestrained explosion in credit and in the resulting liabilities, disclosed and hidden, of the agents in the financial markets. It also occurred in spite of the prescient warnings of a few prominent economists. These were all well-publicized at the time they were made, usually accompanied by derisive and disparaging comments.

In the year or two before the Crisis struck several expert voices warned of the growing fragility of the US and other developed economies and the dangers of a debacle. These voices were not numerous but they were in all cases those of experienced commentators with notable professional careers and high academic qualifications, many of them in positions of high responsibility. The relatively tiny band of wise virgins included:

- Raghuram Rajan,

- William White, of the BIS,

- Wynne Godley (late, and deeply lamented),

- Steve Keen,

- Robert Shiller,

- Nouriel Roubini.

Raghuram Rajan, Chief Economist at the IMF at the time, warned, in 2005 at the central bankers' Jackson Hole conference of that year, of the increased risks resulting from developments in the world's financial markets.

William White, Economic Adviser and Head of Monetary and Economic Development at the Bank for International Settlements, May, 1995 - June, 2008. As early as August, 2003, White warned Alan Greenspan of the dangers of uncontrolled credit. In 2006 he stated 'One hopes that it will not require a disorderly unwinding of current excesses to prove convincingly that we have indeed been on a dangerous path.'

Wynne Godley, now alas deceased and very sorely missed. He first identified the future problems of prevailing macroeconomic policy in January, 1999, in a paper entitled 'Seven Unsustainable Processes'. Later, in April, 2007, in another paper, he predicted the Crisis.

Steve Keen, Economist, presently Honorary Professor of Economics at University College, London. He uttered consistent warnings of a crisis well before the 2008 event. He has also been a sustained critic of the neo-classical macroeconomic models which have for long dominated economic thinking, both in Academia and in the real world of economic policy.

Robert Shiller, presently Professor of Economics at Yale and former chairman of the American Economics Association. He published timely papers predicting both the US stock market bubble of 2001 and the unsustainable housing bubble which led to the 2008 Crisis, reflecting his belief in the 'markets always revert to the mean' principle.

Nouriel Roubini, independent economic adviser and Professor at the Stern School of Business, of NYU, predicted, in an IMF position paper in 2006, the collapse of the US housing market bubble with damaging consequences.

Others who saw the Crisis coming were: **Gary Shilling**, **Peter Schiff**, **Dean Baker, Fred Hansen, Michael Hudson** and **Charles Morrison**.[9]

At the time these warnings were laughed at and peremptorily dismissed and their makers derided as hopelessly out of touch. When **Raghuram Rajan**, then the Chief Economist at the IMF, voiced his misgivings about growing risk in the world's financial markets in a paper presented at the central bankers' Jackson Hole conference in the summer of 2005 entitled 'Has Financial Development made the World Riskier?', he was roundly criticized, not to say ridiculed, and his colleagues at the IMF ignored him. At the time Lawrence Summers even described Rajan as 'slightly Luddite'.

This was the treatment generally handed out to anyone expressing concern at the way things were going and voicing fears of a probable collapse. The prevailing mood in the Golden Age was sunny optimism; 'This time is different!' was the cry and the financial market participants were all making so much money that sceptics were derided as envious nay-sayers, voices crying in the wilderness, to be roundly ignored.

In Academia, the late **Wynne Godley** had earlier foreseen a crisis and presciently modelled its probable evolution. As noted, even earlier **Hyman Minsky** had pointed out the crucial failure of the dominant economic models, including DSGE, to include the financial sector and financial flows in their modelling and calculations. From his analysis of the origins of past crises he concluded that periods of economic stability, if allowed to develop without prudential control, tended naturally and regularly towards financial excess and ultimately to economic crisis and disaster.

Chapter 3: Notes

1. In his biography of Greenspan, 'The Man Who Knew', Sebastian Mallaby suggests strongly that Greenspan was well aware of the dangerous explosion in risk in the US financial markets before the Crisis but did nothing to control it. Greenspan in effect denies this in his record of the Crisis but if Mallaby's suggestion is accurate Greenspan's culpability is the greater.

2. See 'The Slumps that Shaped Modern Finance', The Economist, April 10th, 2014. Also, a recent paper by the IMF provides a thorough analysis and demonstration of the 'unrestrained credit' origins and pathology of historical financial bubbles: (Working Paper WP/18/8: Regulatory Cycles: Revisiting the Political Economy of Financial Crises).

3. In fact, even in the US, this was far from being a new notion. In 1928 Roy Young, then Chairman of the Fed, stated that 'central bankers should be concerned about excessive growth in any line of credit'. Interestingly, McChesney Martin had a distinctly skeptical opinion of the value of Economics and economists. In a recent article in Foreign Affairs, Paul Romer recounts that in 1970 Martin explained to a visitor that although economists asked good questions they worked from the basement at the Fed 'because they don't know their own limitations and they have a far greater sense of confidence in their analyses than I have found to be warranted.'

4. The risks of excessively easy monetary policy were spelled out in a paper by William R. White, issued in August, 2012, by the Federal Reserve Bank of Dallas. 'Ultra-Easy Monetary Policy and the Law of Unintended Consequences: http://www.dallasfed.org/assets/documents/institute/wpapers/2012/0126.pdf

5. Bernanke published his personal record of the Crisis in 2015. The book is a comprehensive record of the Crisis and of the actions taken by the Federal Reserve as it unfolded.

6. Martin Wolf, in his book on the Crisis (The Shifts and Shocks: What We've Learned - and Have Still to Learn - from the Financial Crisis) comments acerbically on Bernanke that 'even two months before the crisis broke .... he had next to no idea what was about to hit him, his institution and the global economy. To be blunt, he was almost clueless.'

7. Greenspan and Ayn Rand. Greenspan and Rand were very close friends until her death in 1982 and he greatly admired her 'philosophy'. Rand's manifesto, The Virtue of Selfishness, is essentially an argument for the unrestrained pursuit of self-interest. (The questionable economic validity of self-interest was even then far from a new thesis: in 1937, F. D. Roosevelt, in his inaugural address, had commented 'We have always known that heedless self-interest was bad morals; we now know that it is bad economics'.)

   As its creator, Rand presented her so-called Objectivist philosophy as the embodiment of realism in human affairs, i.e. as a more empirically valid (and therefore more psychologically realistic and virtuous) world-view than any other political and social ethos. Yet a reading of Rand's two major works of fiction, 'Atlas Shrugged' and 'The Fountainhead', both of which were vehicles for presenting the operation of her 'philosophy' in the real world, makes it clear that at bottom she was a simple utopian and about as far removed from realism (let alone humanity) as it is possible to be.

In the final chapters of 'Atlas Shrugged' Dagney Taggart visits the valley where John Galt lives. The valley is protected by an invisible force-field: it is a sort of magical Shangri-La. The special steel developed by Hank Rearden is described, without explanation, as a 'miracle metal', far out-classing any competitive product.

We are, it is clear, in the utopian, fantasy world of magic and Superman and have left the real world far behind. It is very difficult to understand how such an unrealistic, fairy-tale world-view could come to be regarded as insightful and significant, let alone 'objective'.

8. The full text of the Federal Commission on the Crisis is easily obtainable on the web, e.g. at: https://fcic.law.stanford.edu/report.

9. In a paper published in 2009, 'No One Saw it Coming', Dirk Bezemer, at the University of Groningen, provided a comprehensive record and analysis of the relevant papers of the few who predicted the Crisis.

Chapter 4

WHAT WENT WRONG?
POSTMORTEMS AND LESSONS

A flood of books have been published analyzing and commenting on the many aspects of the Crisis - origins, immediate causes, effects, etc. The books have come from a wide range of experts and commentators, including practicing economists, independent commentators, national institutions like central banks and global institutions like the IMF. The main personalities at the epicenter of the Crisis in the USA have written their memoirs of the event, mostly along the lines of self-justifying excuses for their failure to foresee it. A few macroeconomists have issued their analyses of the Crisis, the reasons for it and their explanations why it was not foreseen. More usefully, there have also been reflective and forward-looking analyses by central bankers/regulators seeking to draw lessons for the future from the debacle.

PART 1: POSTMORTEMS

The books analyzing and commenting on the Crisis fall into two categories:

- expert and relevant analysis,

- breast-beating and excuses.

i) Postmortems: Analysis

Comprehensive analysis of the Crisis, comments on its causes and recommendations for curing its effects are well spelled out in two books:

- **The Shifts and the Shocks – What We've Learned and Have Still to Learn, by Martin Wolf,** and
- **After the Music Stopped, by Alan Blinder.**

Wolf is the FT's chief Economics commentator. His book provides an outstanding, very thorough analysis of the origins and causes of the Crisis. Furthermore, as one of the most experienced and authoritative independent economic journalists alive, his account includes trenchant and appropriate criticism of the Federal Reserve and the US Treasury whose policy failures led to the Crisis. His book has a wide, global scope and includes appropriately acerbic criticism of the competence of the main official players in the drama (**Greenspan, Summers, Bernanke** etc.) and reflections on the theoretical economic origins of the Crisis.

Blinder is a practicing macroeconomist, former Economics adviser to the Clinton White House and former vice-chairman of the US Federal Reserve. His book is mainly a description of the Crisis and its aftermath as it evolved in the USA. He is less ready to blame personalities, all of whom he must know well, and this gives his account a certain sense of the exercise of professional etiquette. As a practicing macroeconomist, Blinder gives a readable professional insider's comment on the Crisis. That said, the really remarkable feature of Blinder's book, particularly one written by an eminent macroeconomist, is his utter failure to address, explain or comment on the part played by the fundamental macroeconomic theory used by Fed. It was the Fed's unyielding faith in its favorite economic model which underlay its complete failure to foresee the Crisis and take steps to prevent it. This, along with the Fed's (i.e.

Alan Greenspan's) uncritical faith in the mantra of 'free unregulated markets', was the theoretical origin of the Crisis.

Tim Geithner is reported as attributing the Fed's failure to 'collective amnesia'. According to him 'There was no memory of what can happen when a nation allows a large amount of risk to build up.' This seems, to put it very mildly indeed, an inexcusable unawareness of financial history, including the recent history of the twentieth century.

ii) Postmortems: Breast-Beating and Excuses

Alan Greenspan and Ben Bernanke, two of the chief culprits, have both written memoirs of the 2008 Crisis:

- **The Map and the Territory,** by **Alan Greenspan**
- **The Courage to Act,** by **Ben Bernanke.**

The chief purpose of both these books is to argue that the two authors bore no responsibility for causing the Crisis. They didn't do it!

Alan Greenspan

Greenspan's book is his personal account of what went wrong and, looking ahead, a forecast of the main economic policy problems facing the USA (demographics, growing social security entitlements, Federal debt). As noted in Chapter 3, for the most part he reiterates and supports, without significant qualification, the principles of neo-classical Economics which induced the Crisis: the belief in the abstraction of rational self-interest as the main driver of human economic decisions (and of economic growth), the inherent tendency of economies to revert to stable equilibrium after a dislocation and, most of all, the dangers of imposing regulations on the operation of free, unfettered markets. He notes the failure of forecasting but is happy to put his faith in the statistical correlations thrown up by historical data. For him, how the economy and the markets reacted to any given set of policies in the past is a reliable guide to how they will react in the future.

What is truly remarkable in his book, just as it is in **Alan Blinder's 'After the Music Stopped'**, is the complete absence of any comment on, let alone serious discussion or consideration of, the dominant DSGE economic model followed by the Fed in analyzing and managing the US economy. Greenspan says that the Fed had more than 250 Economics PhDs when he joined it in 1987 and the institution's website states that the number is now more than 300, plus a very large supporting staff. The consequence of this concentration of firepower has been and remains that the Fed dominates the 'market' in academic economists and therefore in academic Economics[1]. The Fed's failure to foresee, and to take steps to avoid, the potentially disastrous consequences of its free-for-all macroeconomic policies was the chief cause of the Crisis; yet Greenspan's book passes over this crucial factor in silence.

In his biography of **Alan Greenspan**, 'The Man who Knew', **Sebastian Mallaby** implies strongly that Greenspan was well aware of the potentially damaging consequences of the unfettered financial free-for-all regime he presided over. Greenspan's earlier statement, in December, 1996, that the then high valuations of the US equity market showed 'irrational exuberance' seems to confirm that this was true (though the statement was made in the context of Greenspan's querying how a central bank could know reliably that the market was in fact overvalued). If so, his failure to take countermeasures to control the enormous expansion in credit in various forms which in the end triggered the Crisis was a deplorable failure of professional nerve (or perhaps, as Mallaby suggests, a lack of political influence). To his credit, Greenspan has admitted, as have no others among the main actors in the drama, the errors of his judgment and policy actions. Nonetheless, Greenspan's reputation will remain forever tainted by the Crisis.

Ben Bernanke

Ben Bernanke's book, with its grandiose, not to say vainglorious title, is a thorough record of the Crisis from his personal viewpoint as one who was at the epicenter of the Crisis as it developed and unfolded. It can be read in tandem with other 'fly-on-the-wall' reports such as **Andrew Ross Sorkin**'s 'Too Big to Fail'. Yet here again the really remarkable feature of Bernanke's book, as with Greenspan's book and Blinder's, is the utter absence of any mention, let alone discussion, of the dominant theoretical macroeconomic model used by the Federal Reserve - the DSGE model.

Paul Krugman

Paul Krugman published his reflections on the Crisis and on the failure of the Economics profession which it demonstrated in a long article which appeared in the New York Times not long after the Crisis: **How Did Economists Get it So Wrong?**[2] He acknowledges the discrediting of both the Keynesian and the classical monetarist economists by their failure to think outside their abstract theoretical models and the parallel failure of the Efficient Market Hypothesis which had seemed to give support to the view that markets were efficient in pricing assets and should therefore be left free of regulation.[3] He also recognizes the small-scale validity of Behavioral Economics. However, the Crisis showed that the world is inherently much 'messier' than the macroeconomists were able to admit; furthermore the dominant macro model entirely ignored credit.

PART 2: CONFERENCES AND COMMENT

Besides these works, there have been several anthologies of essays by prominent economists commenting from a more theoretical viewpoint on the Crisis and the lessons for economic management to be learned from it.

- Conferences: the IMF, The Economist, Peterson Institute.

- Comment and recommendations for reform.

Conferences

Along these lines the IMF organized after the Crisis a series of conferences devoted to examining it, the reasons for it and potential remedies for the analytical and policy failings which led to it.

The IMF

i) Rethinking Macro Policy II, Getting Granular, What Have We Learned?, April, 2013.

ii) Rethinking Macro Policy III, Progress and Confusion, April, 2015.

iii) Rethinking Macro Policy IV, Evolution or Revolution?, October, 2017 (with the Peterson Institute for International Economics).

Anthologies of the presentations contributed to these conferences have been published under the titles: 'What Have We Learned? , Macroeconomic Policy after the Crisis', published in 2013; 'Progress and Confusion, The State of Macroeconomic Policy', published in 2016; 'Evolution or Revolution?' (in collaboration with the Peterson Institute), published in 2019.

The conferences gathered prominent economists, central bankers, regulators and economic journalists to give their insights into the failures in policy, regulation and economic governance which led to the Crisis and their recommendations for preventing its recurrence and for improving macroeconomic management.

The Economist

An anthology of comments on macroeconomics by that paper's in-house or associate economic journalists was produced by The Economist: 'Economics, Making Sense of the Modern Economy, 2011'.

Peterson Institute for International Economics

The Peterson Institute collaborated with the IMF in organizing the fourth in the series of conferences on Rethinking Economic Policy. The conference was held in Washington in October, 2017. As noted above a book of the proceedings was published in May, 2019, under the title 'Evolution or Revolution?'.

The attenders at these conferences constituted a rollcall of 'the great and the good' elite of macroeconomics and central banking with many of the leading personalities (e.g. **Olivier Blanchard, Lawrence Summers**) present at all four. Until the most recent October, 2017, conference the general tone of the contributions to these conferences was steadily complacent and unruffled. Virtually all the contributions focused on potential refinements of the existing toolkit used in macroeconomic management. They read like recommendations for solving minor problems encountered in the baking of a cake. The pervasive psychological message of the contributors to these earlier conferences amounts to a bland 'Don't worry, this is just a hiccup. We may need to make some minor adjustments but everything is going to be just fine'.[4]

Yet the titles of the conferences give an inkling of growing uncertainty and self-doubt. In 2008, after the Crisis struck, **Olivier Blanchard**, then chief economist at the IMF, was confident enough to affirm 'the state of macro[economics] is good'. The hesitancy implicit in the 'Progress and Confusion' title of the 2015 IMF conference suggests that his former conviction had by then given way to a more qualified assessment of the capabilities of macroeconomists. This growing professional humility was further confirmed in the papers submitted at the October, 2017, conference (where **Blanchard** was co-chairman). The title of the book of the conference papers, published in May, 2019, was 'Evolution or Revolution?'.[5]

Where's the Dominant Model?

Yet again, the remarkable feature of the expert presentations delivered at these conferences is the complete absence of any consideration and criticism of, or even reference to, the disastrous failure of the dominant macroeconomic model used by the Federal Reserve and the other major central banks and finance ministries to manage their economies. This is in spite of the fact that it was the Fed's uncritical faith in this model which laid the groundwork for the Crisis. This omission is extraordinary. It is Hamlet without the Prince. It is as though the official report on the 9/11 destruction of the twin towers in Manhattan contained no reference to Al Qaeda and Osama bin Laden. In this respect the conference reports repeat the similar complete absence of any comment on the DSGE theory by Alan Greenspan, Ben Bernanke and Alan Blinder in their records of the Crisis. As noted, 'economic models' and 'DSGE' do not even have index entries in Bernanke's book. In Greenspan's book 'DSGE' has no index entry and 'model building' rates only a page and a half of text.

Comments from the Trenches

The post-Crisis literature includes noteworthy books by two individuals who were also in the central bank/regulator trenches when the Crisis broke in 2008.

Mervyn King was appointed Governor of the Bank of England in July, 2003, having served earlier as Chief Economist of the Bank; he retired in 2013. He experienced, therefore, the entire Crisis, from its build-up in the 2000s through the Crisis itself to its aftermath. Consequently he was in an outstanding position to judge the full course and significance of the Crisis and to draw lessons for avoiding a new upheaval and for resolving the persistent economic stagnation which the Crisis has induced.

His book, **The End of Alchemy**, is very readable. He combines the considered insights of a skeptical academic economist with the experience of a practicing senior central banker who lived through the world's worst economic crisis since the Great Depression. The main focus of his book is the failure of the structure, operation and regulation of the traditional practice of banking as it has been conducted for centuries. It was this failure, King believes, which enabled the build-up of the imbalances and fragilities which led to the Crisis. He proposes replacing the present orthodoxy, whereby the central bank's lender-of-last-resort power underpins a country's banking system, with a continuous regulatory constraint on the ability of banks to debauch their liquidity ratios (their ability to repay depositors on demand) by engaging in maturity transformation (taking short term deposits and making long-term loans) or otherwise degrading their balance sheets. This transformation, which enables banks to create credit, is the alchemy of his title. He does acknowledge, however, that the making of loans to business has been the basis of economic growth.

Along the way he delivers acute comments on the Eurozone (which he believes to be a social, financial and economic disaster in the making (springing from the trilemma of trying to blend democracy, national sovereignty and economic integration), a problem best resolved by Germany quitting the Euro) and on the decline of the Pax Americana and the US-led global monetary order. He expects another crisis (see below).

As regards economic policy he is decisively in favor of a flexible, 'coping' strategy for dealing with economic upsets rather than adhering more or less strictly to any model. Judgment is the necessary talent. This view is very welcome. Yet, while he does discuss the evolution of Economics since the last World War, his book, like those of Greenspan and Bernanke, fails to acknowledge and address the role in the Crisis played by macroeconomics and specifically by the dominant economic model followed by the major central banks, the Dynamic Stochastic General Equilibrium model. Again, this is Hamlet without the Prince.

Adair Turner was appointed chairman of the UK Financial Services Authority, the body regulating the operation of the banking and financial industry, in September, 2008, days after the collapse of Lehman Brothers and the onset of the Crisis. He held the position for 5 years. His academic background was in Economics and history and his earlier career, after a brief sojourn in banking with Chase Manhattan Bank, included senior posts in various public entities in the UK.

Turner's book, **Between Debt and the Devil**, published in 2016, focuses on the key role in the Crisis played by excess debt and the failure to control it. Unlike Greenspan, Bernanke and King, Turner has critical comments on the Economics profession and the fallacies and failures of the dominant macroeconomic models.

But it is Turner's earlier short book, **Economics after the Crisis**, published in 2012 and based on a series of lectures he gave at the London School of Economics in 2010, not long after the Crisis broke, which is a pointer to a more effective and useful future for macroeconomics. Turner sets out with great clarity and persuasive force the fallacies of the macroeconomic orthodoxy followed by the world's central banks and finance ministries since the early 1980s. In particular he makes the undeniable case for macroeconomics to turn away from its preoccupation with abstract theory bearing no relation to the real world and instead engage fully with human and social needs as they actually are (see Chapter 12). The book should be required reading not only for Economics students but also, more importantly, for politicians and officials who are responsible for formulating economic policy.

Chapter 4: Notes

1. See Chapter 7 for a description of the pernicious effects of this dominance.
2. New York Times, September 6th, 2009.
3. It is a great mystery why the Efficient Market Hypothesis and the related Capital Asset Pricing Model gained the influence they did. If the EMH theory is a statement about anything it is a statement about the behavior of market participants; it says nothing significant about the relationship of market prices to real value (if indeed such a thing is possible).
4. At Conference II, Christine Lagarde suggested, bizarrely, that central banks had emerged as the heroes of the Crisis. In her view the extraordinary actions undertaken by central banks, particularly in the developed economies, probably saved the global economy from a far worse fate than what actually happened. This is probably true but a better assessment of her statement would be that it is like praising someone who digs a deep hole which catastrophically undermines the entire neighborhood for his acute and heroic judgment in deciding not to dig further. Lagarde's statement was reported by Gill Marcus, Governor of the South African Reserve Bank, 2009-2014. As Mr. Marcus commented, 'There seems to be little awareness of what central banks cannot do, as well as what they should in fact not do.' Record of IMF Conference, Progress and Confusion, April, 2015.
5. It is only fair to state that the subtitle of the October, 2017 conference - 'Evolution or Revolution?' - constitutes an admirable acknowledgment of the fallibility of macroeconomists.

Chapter 5

What are Macroeconomists For?

PART 1: THE SOCIAL RESPONSIBILITY OF ECONOMISTS

'As a profession we have made a mess of things.' **Friedrich von Hayek, Nobel Economics Prize Acceptance Lecture,** 1974.

'Much of the past 30 years of macroeconomics has been spectacularly useless at best and positively harmful at worst.' **Paul Krugman**, 2009.

'There is no question that the crisis reflected a major intellectual failure on the part of macroeconomics.' **Olivier Blanchard**, 2017.

'The purpose of studying economics is not to acquire a set of ready-made answers to economic questions but to learn how to avoid being deceived by economists.' **Joan Robinson**.

'Economics is extremely useful as a form of employment for economists.' **J. K. Galbraith**.

If macroeconomists have a use it is to provide governments and central banks with reliable advice in the management of the national economy and the financial system. Keynes' 'General Theory of Employment, Interest and Money', the great man's considered attempt to explain the major factors involved in the operation and management of a developed economy, was written in reaction to the terrible human effects of the Great Depression of the 1920s and '30s. Ever since then Economics and economists have steadily assumed a more and more influential role in the policy-making of governments.

The prosperity of a country and its citizens is the most important factor in their lives and the decisive factor, far outweighing others, when citizens come to cast their electoral votes. It is the key factor deciding the political fate of governments and the success or failure of the careers of government ministers. Consequently, if an economic adviser can recommend policies which successfully deliver growth, politicians and ministers of finance will grant him a large measure of influence and control in economic policy-making.

History is littered with examples of governments kicked out of office because they mismanaged the economy. Bad luck and bad timing obviously play some part in this but electorates, rightly, do not forgive economic incompetence. Since politicians and economists are all too ready to claim credit when things go right, they must take the kicks and the blame when they don't, even if the causal link connecting government policy/ministerial competence to economic success is in fact rather weak.[1]

Economic Advisers: 'Necessary Qualification: Must be Competent'

Given the great importance of their role, economic advisers to governments have a particular responsibility to be competent. What 'competence' means in this case is that if they are to be of any real use, socially or politically, they must be accurate in their analysis and reliable and successful in their advice.

The recent explosion in media coverage has greatly increased public awareness of financial markets, of the global economy and, more pertinently, of the workings of their national economies. As a result finance ministers, central banks and officials are now subject to heightened public attention and accountability and to continuous severe scrutiny, not only from established legislative committees, many of them now routinely televised, but from the great army of professional commentators in think tanks, banks, investment houses and consultancies as well as in Academia. Unlike their predecessors 30-40 years ago, present-day electorates in the developed economies have available to them a continuous stream of varied, informed (and also, of course, uninformed and frankly biased) comment on their government's economic competence. The growth of social media has added to the impact of this heightened media attention.

PART 2: ECONOMIC FORECASTING

'Human beings who spend their time studying the state of the world are poorer forecasters than dart-throwing monkeys.' **Philip Tetlock**, **Expert Political Judgment,** 2005.

'You would do as well to consult an Ouija board as an economist who rigorously follows economic theory when giving advice.' **Steve Keen**, **Debunking Economics.**

'Science is prediction.' Original motto of the **Econometric Society**.

The policy recommendations presented to governments by economic advisers in finance ministries and central banks - and via them to the public at large - are, of course, based on their analysis of the economies they work in and the economic models and theories they believe in. These policy recommendations, on which governments base their regular economic and budget policy statements, are most clearly displayed through the forecasts and predictions of how the major macroeconomic factors (growth, inflation, employment etc.) are expected to change over the next year or two.

Forecasting therefore plays an essential role, both in the formation of economic policy and in its presentation. More importantly, however, it is as good a demonstration as any of the competence of macroeconomists, of the validity of their professional process and therefore of their social usefulness. Unless macroeconomists can demonstrate reliable competence in recommending successful economic policies their social usefulness is slight. In fact, considering their lamentable track record, it would be a very welcome achievement if they simply managed to observe the first precept of the Hippocratic Oath and did no harm.

Economic Forecasting: the Bad, the Worse and the Disastrous

'We really can't forecast all that well; we pretend we can but we really can't.' **Alan Greenspan.**

'The only function of economic forecasting is to make astrology look respectable.' **J. K. Galbraith**.

'The herd instinct among forecasters makes sheep look like independent thinkers.' **Edgar Fiedler**, June, 1977.

'The role of economic forecasts is to show that economists have a sense of humor.' **Herb Stein.**

- **The Record of Failure: The Big Picture**

With the exception of a very few individuals, who were at the time universally ignored or derided for their views (see Chapter 3), the Economics profession failed utterly to foresee the Crisis of 2008. The comprehensively wide extent of this disastrous failure was recorded in an article in the Financial Times of May 30th, 2014, by the FT's Undercover Economist, **Tim Harford**. As Harford reported, out of 77 countries under consideration, 49 were in recession in 2009. The vast majority of economists had not called a single one of these recessions by April, 2008. The economists' collective, ostrich-like unwillingness to entertain the possibility that their complacency as to the health of the global economic and financial system might be disastrously wrong was of course faithfully echoed by the officials and politicians whom they advised and who were in a position to take steps to prevent it.

Since the Crisis moreover, the Economics profession has comprehensively failed to prescribe effective measures for durable economic recovery and a return to historic levels of growth. In the US, since 2009 (i.e. ignoring the collapse after the 2008 Crisis) the economy has recorded average real GDP growth below 2% per annum, barely half the historical average of 3.25%. In February, 2016, the Bureau of Economic Analysis reported that the US economy recorded a 10th straight year of dismal real annual growth at 1.6%. This steady underperformance has continued. In 2017 US growth was 2.2% and in 2019 2.3%.

The stagnation in growth since the 2008 Crisis is a global phenomenon. Significantly lower growth has been recorded in Japan and in the European Union (which continues to be bedeviled by both the strait-jacket of the Euro and the enormous (and basically unbridgeable) social, economic and political differences between Germany and the northern economies, on the one hand, and the southern economies, including France, on the other). According to the WTO, annual growth in world trade slowed from between 5% and 10% in the years before 2007 to about 2% in 2016 and 3% in 2018. Also, world trade as a percentage of global GDP, 25% in 2008, has fallen to 22% and continues to decline. In their October, 2018, report on the global economy the IMF expected persistent stagnation in the advanced economies, with global growth remaining subdued.

The really serious problem is that this miserable performance has been recorded in spite of monetary stimulus (quantitative easing, rock-bottom interest rates, and an unprecedented explosion in public debt) enormously exceeding any previous measures. This contradicts completely the outcome predicted by the macroeconomists' preferred economic model. Since this model was the basis for the forecasts of a rapid return to growth, the result comprehensively demolishes any claim of the macroeconomists to accurate forecasting and, more than this, to any reliable value they may have as policy advisers.

The fact is that the track-record of macroeconomic forecasts produced by the economic departments of official institutions in the developed economies (central banks, finance ministries) has for long been disastrously bad. Examples of this professional incompetence are much too numerous to list but even a cursory inspection of references to forecasts in relevant journals such as the FT, the Wall Street Journal or The Economist, or of the forecasts published regularly by the finance ministries of the developed economies, demonstrates a pretty well continuous record of failure and, what is more, failure by wide margins.

Nor is this just a matter of small, insignificant errors. The forecasting failures, it is true, are not usually as dramatically wide of the mark as the famous statement by **Irving Fisher** in 1929 (that US stock prices 'had reached what looks like a permanently high plateau' days before the Great Crash), but nearly all are badly wrong and often even the fundamental trend, negative or positive, is mistaken.

• The Record of Failure: The Small Picture

This large-scale forecasting failure is matched by a similar failure in much narrower and more specific policy forecasts. In 2012, for example, the Federal Reserve began to publish the views of the members of the Fed's Open Market Committee, the body which discusses and decides US interest rate levels. The members' views on where the federal funds rate should be at the end of 2014 varied from the then prevailing 0-25 basis point range to 2.5% or higher.[2] Enormous divergence on this scale has in fact become the regular pattern. This is about as far as you can get from rifle-shot forecasting precision – and these guys are supposed to be seasoned experts applying the methods of an established science.

These devastating failures put a serious question mark over the fundamental validity of the processes of Economics and in particular over the forecasting methods and practices of the 'science'. It may be, as **Yogi Berra** put it (echoing **Niels Bohr**), that 'it's tough to make predictions, especially about the future' but that is the business professional economists are in - it is the key test of their social usefulness and it is the basis of any respect and attention they deserve.

Finance ministries, even in the major developed economies, have, it is true, some kind of operational excuse, since they serve the governments of their country and cannot be expected to submit analyses or policy recommendations which are significantly at variance with the proclaimed policies and promises of the government of the day and these, for political reasons, tend to be unfailingly positive and optimistic. Nonetheless this excuse, even for finance ministries, does not go very far. Their role and responsibility is to provide independent, valid and reliable advice to the mostly inexperienced politicians who have gained power; acting as puppets and simply parroting opaque technical justifications for the policy prejudices of ministers will not do.

This political excuse applies even less to central banks which are statutorily independent, as they now are in the USA, the UK, the EU and Japan. The forecasting problems facing the Economics departments of the major central banks were discussed in two speeches in the UK by officials of the Bank of England (**Andrew Haldane**, 'Central Bank Psychology', November 17th, 2014, and **Ben Broadbent**, 'Forecast Errors', May 1st,

2013). Both these speeches address the problem of the pretty continuous record of seriously inaccurate forecasting on the part of the Bank of England's Economics department, though it should be said that this lamentable record is widely shared by most other central banks.[3]

This widespread aptitude for erroneous forecasting extends to the major global financial institutions. Thus, the IMF has chalked up a record of seriously inaccurate (and always over-optimistic) forecasting which is second to none. The World Bank's record is no better and the ECB's is quite as bad.[4]

The fair inference to be drawn from this record of continuous and conspicuous failure is not that the economists at central banks and finance ministries are especially incompetent but that the entire process of economic forecasting and the theories and models underlying the forecasts and policy recommendations are, fundamentally and in principle, badly and dangerously flawed.[5]

PART 3: FORECASTING: CONTENT AND PRESENTATION

Nonetheless, in spite of this persistently lamentable track-record, forecasting plays an essential and unavoidable role in the formation of economic policy.[6] In turn this important public role imposes on Economics advisers certain requirements in the formulation and development of economic policy forecasts.

- **Content**

The content of economic policy advice needs to reflect the political requirements of a government presenting its program to its country's electors. To get elected or re-elected, politicians must convince the electors that their program for the economy will significantly improve their lives by boosting growth, generating employment and raising living standards, ideally without inflation. Party manifestos tend not to dwell too much on the detailed specifics of financial policy (changes to the tax code, depreciation rates, balancing the fiscal books, etc.). The essential ingredient is an economic strategy which, it is claimed, will deliver an overall improvement in the living standard of voters, supported by a record of competent management of the national economy.

However, the omission of boring detail in broad-brush manifestos cannot be taken very far. Politicians need to demonstrate credibility. Their policy proposals must convince not only voters but also informed professional critics in the media and Academia that their programs are soundly based. A government economic adviser, however seasoned or academically qualified, who simply tapped his nose and said 'Trust me, my experience tells me that the result of .... will be ....', will not be taken seriously (though there were certainly many occasions during the incumbency of **Alan Greenspan** as Chairman of the US Federal Reserve when his explanations of the policy of the Fed in Congressional hearings led him into realms of opacity which rendered his explanations of Federal Reserve policy Delphic in the extreme).

An economic forecast for public consumption needs to include not only an accurate and dispassionate analysis of the country's existing economic condition but, more importantly, a reasonably detailed forecast of the development of the economy over the next 18-24 months, expressed in terms the public can understand: growth, employment, taxes and allowances, government revenue and expenditure, interest rates and inflation, etc.

These forecasts must appear credible and soundly based. They must be comprehensive, integrating all the significant factors which make up a modern developed economy (consumption, investment, inflation, government finances and taxation, external trade and exchange rates etc., each reflecting very different kinds of economic behavior). To be of any use and to be credible and persuasive an economic forecast needs to incorporate all these factors. It must also include a coherent conception of their interdependence: how and to what extent they interrelate and how changes in any one factor are predicted to impact the others in the short-term - typically, over the next year or so (or until the next election date).

• Presentation

But there is a second important requirement imposed by public economic forecasts. This is presentational. Politicians presenting their economic policies to electorates need to speak with apparent authority. Simply announcing their economic policies in bald statements will not do; the announcements must appear suitably authoritative - as the result not of ad hoc, pragmatic, off-the-cuff, speculative conjecture but of tried and tested intellectual and professional processes. This means in turn that the forecasts which underlie the economic policies presented by the government must appear to be the result of a serious, established, valid and deterministic professional process.

As it happens, this presentational requirement accords very closely and comfortably with the way Economics has developed during the last 60 years. In fact a very cozy symbiosis has developed between the present methods of economists and the need of politicians to appear authoritative to electorates. To be precise, the now dominant use of complex mathematics as the day-to-day language of Economics has enabled economists to seem scientifically authoritative in a way in which the use of plain language would not.[7]

This has had a malign and regrettable result. It has encouraged politicians to feel comfortable in accepting uncritically the recommendations of Economics advisers simply because these advisers now habitually use dense and opaque mathematics to express their theories. From this uncritical acceptance it is a short step to using these recommendations as the basis for policy advice.

PART 4: ECONOMIC FORECASTING:
THE MACROECONOMICS CONFIDENCE TRICK

As it now works in practice, the consequence of the now pervasive use of mathematics by economists is a two-level confidence trick. First, politicians are led to accept uncritically the abstract theories of professional economists. They are bemused by, and accept at the advisers' own professional estimation and without serious question, the authority of advisers speaking an opaque and mysterious mathematical lingo. Secondly, the 'expertise' of these economists, assumed as validated by their use of complicated mathematics, is in turn adopted by politicians to persuade electorates that they know what they are doing. The result is that electorates are gulled into accepting apparently 'expert' statements as authoritative and reliable.

The basis of this deception lies in the pretense that the use of complicated mathematics gives economic models and theories validity. The psychological rationale of the deception goes as follows: 'this explanation is mathematical and very complicated, therefore it must be precise; if it's precise it must be accurate; if it's accurate then it must be valid and if it's valid then it can reliably be used as a basis for policy recommendations.'

This is obviously fallacious, delusional and dangerous. Equally obviously, it suits politicians admirably, giving their policy statements the apparent authority of independent, expert, professional validation.

Unfortunately, economists themselves are also victims of the deception; they are encouraged to continue believing that their abstract mathematical gymnastics has some real social use.

The disastrous effect of this confidence trick was perfectly illustrated by the uncritical respect accorded to **Alan Greenspan** during his tenure of the Chairmanship of the Federal Reserve. His testimonies to Congress during his Chairmanship of the Fed were famous for their opacity and for the reverential respect they received.[8]

Bad Mathematics

A further problem, besides the failure of mathematics to generate successful economic advice, is that there are intrinsic fallacies in the way mathematics is used in economic theorizing, modelling and forecasting (see Chapter 6).

Game Over

This confidence trick is at last coming under fire. First, there is now experimental evidence that the use of complex and seemingly expert language generates a matching suspension of critical thinking in the human brain.[9] Secondly, this deception has (finally, after more than 70 years of intensifying obfuscation), been acknowledged by a respected member of the Economics profession. **Paul Romer**, an economist of incontestable academic repute, has set out the fallacies of the reliance on mathematics (and the corresponding fallacies in Economics and economic management) in a speech delivered in January, 2016, '**The Trouble with Macroeconomics**'.[10]

Chapter 4: Notes

1. Examples of politicians falling prey to the consequences of economic mismanagement (or, of course, unlucky business-cycle timing) are legion. In recent

history, GHW Bush lost the US presidential election in 1992 to Bill Clinton after hiking taxes in spite of his ringing 'no new taxes…read my lips' declaration at the Republican Convention that year. In the UK, John Major was defeated in the 1997 general election after the earlier ignominious withdrawal of Sterling from the European Exchange Rate Mechanism in 1993. More recently, Gordon Brown lost the UK General Election of 2010 to David Cameron following the Labour Party's comprehensive mismanagement of the UK economy during his premiership. The election of new boy Emmanuel Macron in France came as the country had staggered along for years with near-zero growth and more than 10% unemployment. Both the established political parties – the French Socialist party and the Centre-Right – have suffered the extreme penalty for economic incompetence.

2. According to Alan Blinder, only two members said that the near-zero interest-rate policy should continue into 2016 though this is in fact what happened. Alan Blinder, After the Music Stopped, 2013.

3. The candid admission, by Andy Haldane, Chief Economist at the Bank of England, on January 5th, 2017, of the failure of the economics profession to foresee the 2008 Crisis is a prime example. His words were: 'It is a fair cop to say that the profession is in some degree in crisis.'

   Other comments on this failure include 'Economic Forecasters Failing Vision', Chris Giles, FT, November 25th, 2008, on the failure of the Fed, the ECB, the Bank of England and the IMF, and 'Thinking Outside the Bank', the Buttonwood column in The Economist, November 22nd, 2014.

4. These failures are regularly noted and commented on in the financial press (see for example The Economist, Free Exchange, January 9th, 2016, 'Despite fore-casters' best efforts, growth is devilishly hard to predict').

5. A measure of the extent of forecasting uncertainty and of its resulting inac-curacies can be gained by studying the wide range of the upper and lower limits of possible outcomes in the forecast fan charts presented by finance ministries and central banks for even short-term predictions of how the main economic factors of an economy are expected to develop. Also, if you are led to think that this proneness to forecasting error is the unique preserve of central banks and finance ministries, you should read the wildly divergent and inaccurate forecasts of the major eco-nomic factors of the US economy (growth, interest rates, employment, inflation etc.) for the coming year, issued regularly in December each year by investment banks, investment managers and economic consultants. These are collated and pub-lished regularly in financial journals. Or, to take a more up-to-date example, check the almost universal faulty predictions of an imminent and significant rise in US interest rates which have been staple year-end fare in the predictions by banks and investment managers in the financial press for several years.

6. Alan Greenspan is on record as believing that forecasting is 'an inbred necessity of human nature'.

7. Keynes, who had a superb talent for clarity of expression, was an exception to this rule.
8. John McCain, nobody's fool, stated, in October, 2008 (though, to be fair, it was in an election meeting), that if Alan Greenspan died 'we should prop him up, put dark glasses on him and pretend he was still alive'.
9. See, for example, J. Engelmann, C. M. Capra, C. Noussair and G. Berns: 'Expert Financial Advice Neurobiologically "Offloads" Financial Decision-Making under Risk', PLoS One, March 24th, 2009.
10. His speech was afterwards issued as a paper in The American Economist. His paper is a thorough and comprehensive demolition of the use of mathematics by the economics profession. It amplifies and extends Romer's earlier paper criticizing the 'slipshod, imprecise quasi-maths' in academic economics in an article in the American Economic Review, 'Mathiness in the Theory of Economic Growth', American Economic Review, May, 2015. See Chapter 6 for a fuller comment.

Chapter 6

MATHEMATICS: WAS KEYNES A MUGGLE ?

'95% of Economics is common-sense – made to look difficult with the use of jargon and mathematics.' **Ha-Joon Chang, Economics: The User's Guide,** 2014.

'Too large a proportion of recent 'mathematical' economics are mere concoctions, as imprecise as the initial assumptions they rest on, which allow the author to lose sight of the complexities and interdependencies of the real world in a maze of pretentious and unhelpful symbols.' **J. M. Keynes, The General Theory of Employment, Interest and Money,** 1936. (his apostrophes)

'40 years of investment in mathematising economics has made it less acceptable among economists to admit ignorance of mathematics than to admit ignorance of history.' **Deirdre McCloskey, The Secret Sins of Economics,** 2002.

'A convenient consequence of the systematic use of complex mathematics to propound economic theories is to protect those theories from criticism from the uninitiated.' **Steve Keen, Debunking Economics,** 2011.

PART 1: ECONOMICS AND MATHEMATICS

The adoption of mathematics as the universal language of Economics has been the defining feature of the development of the subject over the last half-century. These days, if you open any of the current leading economic journals you will find it filled with pages of the mathematical equations and formulae which have become the day-to-day jargon of professional economists.[1] **Richard Thaler**, the behavioral economist awarded the Nobel Economics Prize in 2017, attributes the start of the invasion of economic thinking by mathematics to the 1941 PhD thesis of **Paul Samuelson** at Harvard, **'Foundations of Economic Thought'**. According to **Thaler**, Samuelson's thesis 'redid all of economics with what he considered to be proper mathematical rigor.[2] Earlier, **Joseph Schumpeter** had acknowledged the psychological attraction of mathematics in Economics.[3]

Since Samuelson's paper, and **'Foundations of Economic Analysis'** the book which sprang from it, but especially over the last 50 years as the explosive advances in computer power from the 1970s onwards enabled the quick and easy exploration of complicated economic models, professional economists have chosen to express in mathematical terms their theories and models of how economies work and their economic predictions and policy recommendations. The relationships between the many factors which combine to make up a modern developed economy are now habitually expressed by professional economists in complex equations, a set of these equations, taken together, making up a theoretical model of the economy (or, at a lower level, of a subsidiary economic process).

As a result mathematics has now taken over academic Economics. Present-day economists are encouraged to avoid the use of plain language in describing their economic theories and models and to resort instead to complex mathematics unaccompanied by any plain-language explanation (or even a plain-language summary of the argument and the economic factors involved).

No Mathematics, No Career

The present dominance of mathematics in Economics has had another pernicious consequence: competence in econometric mathematics is now the necessary precondition of a successful career as a professional economist. In the 1995 words of **Deirdre McCloskey** quoted at the head of this chapter, '40 years of investment in mathematising economics has made it less acceptable among economists to admit ignorance of mathematics than to admit ignorance of history'.[4]

In the longer history of Economics the now universal move into mathematics is a recent phenomenon. **Adam Smith**, in **'The Wealth of Nations'**, published in 1776, set out a theory of economic behavior in plain prose with no recourse to mathematical formulae. **John Stuart Mill**, another early thinker on economic behavior, also avoided mathematics entirely. **J.M. Keynes**, in his great work **'The General Theory of Employment, Interest and Money'**, used very little algebra to illustrate his arguments.

Both **Keynes** and **Alfred Marshall**, another of the 'founding fathers' of Economics, were profoundly critical of the use of mathematics by economic theorists, yet Keynes was himself a mathematician of high repute. Besides Keynes' dismissive opinion quoted at the head of this chapter, Marshall, who was also a respected mathematician, had this to say about the use of mathematics in Economics:

'(1) Use mathematics as a shorthand language rather than as an engine of enquiry,

(2) Keep to the mathematics till you have done,

(3) Translate into English,

(4) Then illustrate by examples that are important in real life,

(5) Burn the mathematics,

(6) If you can't succeed in (4), burn (3).'

Marshall and Keynes scrupulously subordinated their use of mathematics, sparing as it was, to plain-language economic description. Even more importantly, they never lost sight of the inherent variability of economic behavior and the resulting inherent uncertainty of economic judgments and theories. The difference in approach, clarity and intellectual honesty between their firm subordination of mathematics to plain description in Economics and the now universal rejection of clear explanation and expression in favor of complex, obfuscating mathematics, could not be more stark.[5]

Was Keynes a Muggle?

The dominance of mathematics is of course strongly endorsed by leading professional and academic economists. Thus, **Greg Mankiw**, presently Professor of Economics at Harvard and former chairman of the Council of Economic Advisers to President George W. Bush, regards all non-economists as 'mere Muggles', in spite of the poor (not to say, in recent history, disastrous) record of economists like himself in managing the US economy.

He insists that knowledge of advanced mathematics is an absolute essential for any aspiring economist. 'Take mathematics courses until it hurts', he recommends. **Mankiw** regards a failure to master complex mathematics as the key intellectual deficiency of those he describes as 'Muggles' (with of course the corollary implication that, in spite of their calamitous track record managing real economies, non-Muggle economists are all-knowing and all-powerful wizards).

No Improvement in Performance

Unfortunately for **Prof. Mankiw** and his colleagues in the Economics profession (who have essentially included, in the USA, every recent member of the President's Council of Economic Advisers, plus the Chairman of the Fed and the Chief Secretary to the US Treasury, i.e. everyone with any significant economic influence) the experience of the US economy over the last two decades, with the internet crisis of 2000 and the vastly worse Crisis of 2008, provides overwhelming evidence that the explosive growth in the use of mathematics in Economics has done nothing to improve economic management or the quality of the recommendations of economic advisers like himself.

The reason is not, obviously, because mathematics is intrinsically suspect but because economists have thoroughly perverted its use. In fact, so far from improving macroeconomic management, the consequences of the dominance of mathematics in Economics have been for the most part seriously negative.

Economic History: No Thanks!

'Outsiders would be amazed at the Historical Ignorance of the economist. [You would] think that the scientific evidence about economies before the past few years would surely figure in an economist's data. It doesn't.' **Deirdre McCloskey, The Secret Sins of Economics, 2002,** (her capitals).

In close lock-step with the mathematical take-over of Economics came a steady move towards the elimination of the study of economic history in Economics courses. This trend became pervasive. As Deirdre McCloskey, Professor of Economics and History at the University of Illinois, Chicago, reports, 'One graduate program after another in the 1970s and '80s cut the requirement that students become familiar with the economic past'.

She records that PhDs from her then university, the University of Chicago, 'sent economic history to the guillotine' after she left in 1980 and the universities of Harvard, Princeton, Minnesota and Columbia took similar action shortly afterwards. Note, too, that this cut was for graduate students, who might be presumed to need a wider and deeper understanding of cause and effect in Economics.

The result is that today's Economics students gain no historical perspective on how past economic policy has worked out in practice. This lack of interest in, not to say unwillingness to be aware of, what happened in the past is particularly damaging in Economics. Economic history is a record of the results of past attempts to solve the most important social problems, problems such as creating growth and reducing poverty, which have bedeviled human history for centuries. Economics is the area of public policy which affects human well-being most closely. Ignorance of the effects of past economic policies and the resulting ignorance of the insights from studying these is a serious and severe limitation on the competence of economic advisers.

Economics Textbooks

Samuelson's book, which rapidly became the standard text book for undergraduate Economics courses, is still in regular use. It was written more than 70 years ago and with its help unrealistic Economics has conquered the world. Although Samuelson's abstract, mathematical method is still dominant, the years since his book have seen the growth and development of a considerable variety of alternative theories about the operation and management of developed economies (see Chapter 8).

You would expect, therefore, that the scope of academic textbooks for Economics students would have evolved and expanded in parallel with the vigorous and diverse development of economic thinking since Samuelson. It is consequently depressing to see that, in the US at least, current popular text books for Economics undergraduates continue to define Economics, as did Samuelson, as the interplay of a series of abstract equations.

This analytical method remains the dominant intellectual framework for the academic teaching of Economics. Three of the most popular current textbooks for first degree Economics students demonstrate this intellectual inertia. **'The Principles of Macroeconomics'** by **William Baumol and Alan Blinder**, a textbook by **Gregory Mankiw** with the same title and **'Macroeconomics'** by **Olivier Blanchard**, all follow to the theoretical letter the Samuelson prototype, with the addition of jocular comments and examples. It is now more than 70 years since the publication of **Samuelson's 'Foundation of Economic Analysis'** yet students of Economics are still reared on the unrealistic abstractions first set out by Samuelson.

PART 2: MATHEMATICS: FLAWS AND LIMITATIONS

Flaws

The chief consequences of the universal resort to mathematics in Economics have been pervasive opacity and obscurity and, above all, a steady drift away from the real world towards empty and useless abstraction.

- **Opaque complexity**: the Economics profession has deliberately obscured the workings and results of its processes behind a smoke-screen of mathematics, masquerading as analytical rigor.

- **Abstraction**: the Economics profession has retreated behind this mathematical smokescreen to pursue abstract theoretical exercises which have little or no relation to the real world.

Opaque Complexity

Here is an equation:

$$\ln\left\{\lim_{\delta\to\infty}\left\{[(X')^{-1} - (X^{-1})'] + \frac{1}{\delta}\right\}\right\} + (\sin^2 q + \cos^2 q)$$
$$= \sum_{n=0}^{\infty} \frac{\cosh p\sqrt{1 - \tanh^2 p}}{2^n}$$

This is how, if you are one of today's economists, you express the simple mathematical statement 1+1=2.[6]

The equation shown above may be an exaggerated example but it illustrates well the prevailing practice in the world of Economics.

Abstraction: 'Goodbye Real World!'

'If you believe that you can use unreality to model reality then eventually your grip on reality itself can become tenuous.' **Steve Keen, Debunking Economics**.

'No reality, please. We're economists.' **Mark Blaug.**

'Economists, by and large, do not study the workings of the actual economic system. They theorize about it.' **Ronald Coase.**

'Rather than …. acknowledging that the foundations of Economics are unsound and must therefore be changed, most mathematical economists are …. so ignorant of the real world that they invent some fudge to disguise the gaping hole they have discovered in the theory.' **Steve Keen, Debunking Economics**.

The adoption of mathematics as the language of Economics encouraged and reinforced the intellectual and professional shift away from plain language and the real world towards the unreal, abstract world of theorems and equations. **Paul Samuelson**, in '**Economics**', his textbook for undergraduate Economics students, first published in 1948 and revised and reissued many times since, was the first to explain Economics as, essentially, a comprehensive body of abstract equations and graphs: Demand/Supply, Marginal Profit/Cost, etc. The professional shift which the wide circulation of Samuelson's book encouraged and propelled was a fundamental move in economic theory away from the real world and into systematic abstraction. The disastrous consequences of this shift are with us still.

Limitations

'Conventional economics has abused mathematics in two main ways: by practicing bad mathematics and by not acknowledging the limitations of mathematics.' **Steve Keen, Debunking Economics.**

The lamentable track-record of economists in forecasting and in the advice they give is a matter of public record - the Crisis of 2007/8 is decisive proof - but besides this the adoption of mathematics as the preferred language of Economics has consequences. Mathematics imposes constraints on much of the analysis and many of the calculations which economists make and on the economic models they devise. Like any language, mathematics has its own grammar and rules of usage. These are rigorous and incontestable, as grammatical rules typically are, and they set well-defined limits to the validity and relevance of mathematics in Economics and to its usefulness as a means of expressing theories of economic behavior.[7]

Mathematics is the language of the natural, 'hard' sciences. The theories and formulae of physics, chemistry, astronomy and the other natural sciences are expressed mathematically; doing so makes statements precise and enables the empirical testing of theoretical predictions against real life results. As a result the natural sciences accumulate a steadily growing body of valid explanations of how the world works, confirmed by rigorous testing.

Describing a new scientific theory in precise mathematical terms allows the theory to be tested, and proven or disproven, against empirical evidence. Thus the existence of the Higgs boson, predicted in 1964 by **Peter Higgs**, was confirmed in 2012 as the particle, with the characteristics predicted by him, was observed. Compare this disciplined exercise with the lamentable track-record of macroeconomists in forecasting the results of economic policies even one year into the future.

This sort of rigorous and reliable predictability has always been the goal of Economics and economists have always aspired to and envied the authoritative status of the predictive process in the hard sciences. Consequently there is for economists an inherent appeal in using mathematics to express theories of economic behavior. Mathematics lends a desirable 'scientific' gloss to economic theorizing and encourages economists to believe that the theories and models which they develop have the status of discoveries as valid as those of the 'hard', natural sciences. This belief is baseless.[8]

There are two major economic factors impacted by the limits to the usefulness of mathematics:

- **Quantification**
- **Nonlinear Dynamic Equations: Unstable Solutions.**

QUANTIFICATION

'In the social sciences often what is treated as important is that which happens to be accessible to measurement.' **Friedrich Hayek, Nobel Economics Prize acceptance speech,** 1974.

'Economists would rather focus on things they can measure.' **George Akerlof and Robert Shiller, Animal Spirits,** 2009.

'The sciences are full of measurements which ... can be regarded as constants; there are no such constants in economics. ... The economic world ... is inherently in a state of flux.' **John Hicks, Causality in Economics,** 1979.

'Given the complex relationship between economic factors that can't be quantified and those that can, the application of mathematical methods to those that can is nearly always a waste of time.' **Alfred Marshall**, reported by **A. L. Bowley,** 1901.

If you've chosen to use mathematical equations and models to express your analysis of how a complex economy works and to use this analysis to make policy recommendations and predictions about the effect of economic policies, the values you use for the factors you're dealing with need to be accurate. Unless the values for these factors are reliable, using mathematics to define an economic model and express the relationships between the real economic variables (growth, inflation, employment, etc.), and how they change over a given period, is a futile exercise.

A crucial difference between the 'hard' sciences and Economics is that many of the values found in the 'hard' sciences are constants. The speed of light, absolute zero, gravity, the boiling point of water (subject to air pressure) have constant values; they are not dependent on the different and continuously shifting opinions of observers. Economics has no such constant values. The factors economists need to measure are the responses of human agents to a range of factors which are very diverse. These responses are impossible to measure with the reliable accuracy which would make their models and predictions testable, realistic and useful.

Furthermore the behavior, choices and motives of economic agents are subject to unceasing change, not only independently but in continuous reaction to events and to the behavior of other agents. So it is not only reliable basic data for these factors which economists need to have but data on changes in all of them and how these changes, again, interact with each other.

The different forms of economic behavior which the factors represent are almost infinitely variable, not only intrinsically and over time-periods varying from very short-term to long-term, but also in continuous reaction to the shifting values of the many other factors involved. Reliable predictions based on such shifting ground are impossible; to pretend otherwise is simply dishonest.[9]

How Long *is* a Piece of String?: GDP

An example of the difficulty Economics faces in delivering realistic, useful results is the measurement of economic growth. When economists talk about economic growth they are typically talking about measuring changes in gross domestic product (GDP). Measurements of GDP are measurements of the productive performance of an economy. GDP is the measure of economic activity which the public (and the financial markets) have learned to accept as the major indicator of growth. Good positive figures for GDP are accepted as evidence of successful economic management by an incumbent government.

Yet the entire concept of GDP is uncertain. A recent book by the economist **Diana Coyle, 'GDP, A Brief but Affectionate History',** describes the numerous different definitions of GDP, the different methods of measuring it and the wide variations which result. For example: how do you measure accurately the economic value of services, which now make up the major part of developed economies? Furthermore, official GDP data are baldly economic: they take no account of major factors which can strongly affect the quality of life such as environmental pollution or significant economic inequality. Yet small changes in the announced value of GDP quarter-by-quarter trigger big moves in global financial markets which immediately impact the investment and credit markets and in turn the lives of you and me.

It is not just that obtaining a reasonably accurate figure for the total economic output of a developed economy measuring in US$ trillions is extremely difficult in itself. The experience of the US economy during the past few years and the way it impacts monetary policy decisions by the Federal Reserve provides a good example of the narrow margins for error within which economic decisions are made. To suppose that a decision by the Fed to raise the Fed Funds rate by 0.25% is an exercise in precise, relevant and expert economic management is simple fantasy, however much the Fed's Open Market Committee cloak their proceedings in elaborate language.

No More Business Cycles

It is true that before the Crisis of 2008 the monetary task of the Fed (and of the central banks in most other developed economies) was simpler. The growth/inflation cycles were reliably regular and the correspondingly appropriate interest rate policy was much more easily predictable. This relatively predictable pattern disappeared after the 2008 Crisis. Since the Crisis the US (along with the other major developed economies) has sputtered along without displaying any recognizable cyclical trends in a sort of low-intensity 'steady state' condition which has been characterized (by the economist and former official **Larry Summers**) as 'secular stagnation'.

There are many theories as to the fundamental origins of this condition. These include: the absence of any pick-up in **Keynes'** 'animal spirits' on the part of business entrepreneurs, the increasing adoption of Artificial Intelligence and robotics in industrial production and the corresponding steady elimination of unskilled jobs, the still enormous overhang of debt both private and public and the decidedly more risky geopolitical and global economic scene.

This has left the Federal Reserve (and the other major central banks, except the Bank of Japan) in a quandary. Their solution to the Crisis - massive monetary stimulus - has, against all expectations, failed to return economic growth in the US (and also in Europe and Japan) durably to its historical trend level. Following the disastrous experience of the 1970s, the overriding need to guard against inflation has been a major corner-stone of monetary policy. For some time after the Crisis this concern was replaced by a fear of incipient deflation and even now inflation in the US economy still remains at a level which is unusually low and not explicable by the usual tools. The economic statistics on the US economy have continued to be very disappointing for several years.

There are therefore no clear indicators to what monetary policy the Fed should follow or what guidance they should give for future monetary policy. This uncertainty has been reflected in the Fed's indecision about raising interest rates throughout the last few years and in the precisely non-committal language it has used to explain its monetary policy.[10]

NO STABLE SOLUTIONS: NON-LINEAR DYNAMIC EQUATIONS

The macroeconomist has another troublesome methodological prob-lem. Any useful and realistic theory of how a developed economy works has to include a large number of different factors. If it is to be of any real use a macroeconomic model needs to specify reliably the interaction and interdependence of a large number of very different variables: investment, unemployment, credit, interest rates, taxation, imports and exports, the exchange rate, inflation etc. Besides the prob-lem of measuring these factors reliably (see **Quantification** above), the macroeconomist needs to specify how they relate to each other. He (or she, though it happens that there are fewer female than male macro-economists and indeed, *pace* the eminently deserving **Joan Robinson**, only two female winners of the Nobel Economics Prize) must specify a model of how the many factors interact. These models are expressed in terms of equations specifying how the variable factors affect each other.

The problem economists have is that multi-factor equations handling more than two interdependent variables generate unstable solutions – the results are undeterministic. Once there are more than two variables in a system of non-linear differential equations, there is in fact no stable solution. What this means is that it is not possible to devise models which include all the necessary variable factors and which deliver comprehensive, useful and realistic economic forecasts.[12]

Thus Economics faces two fundamental and crucial problems: first, the impossibility of measuring reliably the actions of economic agents and secondly, the impossibility of devising economic models which are able to deal usefully with more than a very few (i.e. two) of the economic factors whose interaction you need to demonstrate.

These are very serious problems: what is the point of your model if it is unable to determine convincingly how the many factors in a complex modern economy affect each other? If your models are unable to deliver valid results they are of little use in devising relevant policy measures; furthermore they may well be badly misleading.

Solution: Simplify, Reduce and Eliminate

'The theoretical economy is often assumed to be deterministic as results are usually easier to obtain under this assumption.' **Clive Granger, The Philosophy of Economic Forecasting,** 2012.

Economists have resorted to two expedients to 'solve' this problem; both expedients enable 'solutions' by simplifying the conditions. The first solution preferred by economists to the lack of reliable data is simply to assume values (often based on statistics) for factors for which there are no reliable data or, alternatively, to reduce and restrict the definition of the relevant factor until it is so simple as to be completely unrealistic and unrepresentative of any actual, verifiable behavior. The second is simply to reduce the scope of the problem until it becomes solvable by ordinary equations.

A macroeconomic model of a developed economy, if it is to be useful, will need to calculate the interdependency of many very different factors. In practice, given the indeterminacy limitations described above, 'solution' of a model's equations is only possible if a large number of substantive assumptions are made. Furthermore the necessary assumptions include assumptions about economic causation. The obvious problem with these methodological shifts and expedients is that, separately or together, they nullify the validity of both the economists' professional process and the 'solutions' which they generate.

PART 3: HOW MATHEMATICS HAS CORRUPTED ECONOMICS

Macroeconomists therefore face the problem that there are severe limits to using mathematics to get valid and testable solutions to their models of how the many economic factors in a developed economy relate to each other. On the other hand, however, mathematics delivers some impressive and desirable presentational benefits.

Mathematics: the Presentational Benefit

Besides deflecting critical skepticism of their competence and relevance, the systematic use of abstract mathematics as the language of

Economics has, for economists, the great merit of delivering two very significant presentational and professional benefits.

- **The Appearance of Scientific Rigor**

The first great benefit is to give the appearance of scientific rigor and authority to the theories expressed in an economic model, particularly if the mathematics is elaborate and complicated. The audience for Economics advisers, whether politicians or the general public, can reliably be assumed to have only a rudimentary grasp of mathematics. Calculus is likely to be 'terra incognita' to them. The natural psychological consequence of this unfamiliarity is an uncritical acceptance of, even reverence for, the presumed expertise of anyone presenting a policy recommendation supported by complicated mathematics.

- **The Elite Economics Priesthood**

'Economists act very much like a guild. ... The guild mentality renders the profession insular and immune to outside criticism. The models may have problems but only card-carrying members of the profession are allowed to say so.' **Dani Rodrik, Economics Rules**.

'A convenient consequence of the systematic use of complex mathematics to propound economic theories is to protect those theories from criticism from the uninitiated.' **Steve Keen, Debunking Economics.**

'The vast majority of economists believe that this high caste, the mathematical economists, did their work properly and proved that the theory is internally consistent.' **Steve Keen, Debunking Economics.**

The second benefit delivered by the use of complicated mathematics is the enormous merit of elevating the collective set of practicing academic economists from a bickering crowd of pretentious impostors into a select group of initiates with privileged access to the mysteries, insights and wisdom of sophisticated economic thinking. The use of elaborate and complex mathematics delivers the desirable effect of erecting a barricade of opacity against the vulgar scepticism of the ignorant, uninitiated, mathematically-challenged mob (i.e. the general public - you and me) whom **Greg Mankiw** despises as 'mere Muggles'.

Behind their mathematical barricade economists continue to indulge in sterile, vacuous skirmishing of negligible utility, brandishing irrelevant theoretical abstractions against each other, safe in the knowledge that the general public (and their political masters) are incapable of understanding them and that their professional colleagues are too committed to comfortable careers playing the same game to rock the boat.

PART 4: THE GREAT ECONOMICS CONFIDENCE TRICK

The fact is that a dispassionate observer, viewing the development of the Economics profession over the last 60 years or so and noting the increasing dominance of opaque, abstract and irrelevant theory and seeing the parallel track-record of successive policy stumbles and failures[12], culminating in the global Crisis of 2008, would have difficulty not to conclude that the defects outlined above have been systematically used by economists to perpetrate an egregious confidence trick.

A key article of the economists' faith and a key process in their analytical method is that statistical data for the past behavior of economies is a reliable guide to their future behavior[13]: we can be confident that tomorrow will be reliably like yesterday. As **Alan Greenspan** states, in his book on the Crisis '**The Map and the Territory**', economists base their projections of future economic behavior on data for what happened in the past. The term for this is 'regression analysis'. For Greenspan 'regression analysis has turned out to be one of the most effective tools for divining economic cause and effect.'[14] How economic agents behaved in the past is for economists a reliable guide to how they will respond in the future.

This is essentially a fundamental belief in inertia as the governing principle in human economic responses. When you combine this with economists' use of complicated and opaque mathematics and the respect given to economists in their role as economic advisers, it seems not unfair to sum up the achievements of macroeconomics over the last 60 years as an exercise in **'Elaborate Inertia Masquerading as Expert Foresight'.**

At last: No More Smoke and Mirrors

Happily, this deception has (finally, after more than 70 years of intensifying obfuscation) been acknowledged by a respected senior member of the Economics profession. As noted, **Paul Romer**, an economist of impeccable repute (see his bio in Wikipedia) has set out the fallacies of the reliance on mathematics (and the resulting fallacies in Economics and macroeconomic management) in a recent paper (**The Trouble with Macroeconomics, September, 2016**)[15]. It is worth quoting in full the Abstract of the paper:

'For more than three decades macroeconomics has gone backwards. The treatment of identification now is no more credible than in the early 1970s but escapes the challenge because it is so much more opaque. Macroeconomic theorists dismiss mere facts by feigning an obtuse ignorance about such simple assertions as "tight monetary policy can cause a recession". Their models attribute fluctuations in aggregate variables to imaginary causal forces that are not influenced by the action that any person takes. A parallel with string theory from physics hints at a general failure mode of science that is triggered when respect for highly regarded leaders evolves into a deference to authority that displaces objective fact from its position as the ultimate determinant of scientific truth.'

Professional Doubts

Besides **Paul Romer**'s comprehensive criticism of the use of mathematics in macroeconomics noted above there are additional signs from senior figures within Economics and in the wider world that the failings of their profession are giving rise to misgivings as to its health and relevance.

Edmund Phelps (Nobel Economics Laureate, 2006), in a paper entitled **'The Three Revolutions Economics Needs'**, summarizing a recent speech, identifies three deficiencies: imperfect knowledge (the failure to deal with uncertainty, as distinct from risk); imperfect information (the wide variation in knowledge, understanding and therefore economic consequence between economic agents) and economic dynamism (the lack of a valid theory of economic growth).[16]

Fareed Zakaria, in an article **'The End of Economics'** recently published in the magazine Foreign Policy, Winter 2019 issue, believes the intellectual hegemony enjoyed by Economics since the end of the Cold War is over.[17] (Lawrence Summers, in a posting in his blog, naturally disputes Zakaria's conclusion.)

Chapter 6: Notes

1. The adoption of mathematics as the 'language' of Economics had its origins in the nineteenth century in the works of the French economist Leon Walras (1834-1910) and the English economist William Jevons. Their Wikipedia entries summarize their contributions to the development of Economics. Their discoveries of the use of mathematics in Economics were independent of each other. Walras developed a 'science' of Economics based on the application of differential calculus (he also, even more regrettably, adopted the theory of economic equilibrium as the state towards which the actions of economic agents naturally tend, (see Chapter 7)).

Interestingly, Walras had earlier made scathing reference to 'economists who do not know any mathematics' in spite of having himself twice failed entry to the Polytechnique School in Paris because of his weakness in Maths. He clearly experienced a Saul-to-Paul conversion, because in his 1909 paper 'Economics and Mathematics' he was one of the first (of very, very many) to argue that the mathematical statements of economics were as valid as those of the physical sciences. Jevons major work was entitled 'A General Mathematical Theory of Political Economy'.

2. The economist Kenneth Boulding commented 'Mathematics brought rigor to economics. Unfortunately it also brought mortis'.

3. 'For as long we are unable to put our arguments into figures, the voice of our science, although occasionally it may help to dispel gross errors, will never be heard by practical men.' Joseph Schumpeter, 1933.

4. See: 'The Use of Mathematics in Economics and its Effect on a Scholar's Academic Career.' Espinosa, Rondon and Romero, September, 2012.

5. The critical quotes about mathematics in Economics at the head of this chapter are the tip of a large iceberg. Thus, for Yanis Varoufakis, recently Greece's Economics Minister, present-day economic thinking is no better than 'thinly disguised forms of mathematised superstition which have managed to dominate theory and policy.'

6. I am indebted to James Montier, of the investment firm Grantham, Mayo, van Otterloo (GMO), for this happy quote.

7. Chapter 16 of Keen's book, Debunking Economics, 'Don't Shoot Me, I'm only the Piano', presents the detailed reasons why it is not mathematics itself but the way it is used in Economics which is problematic.

8. It may be the case that the relationships between several variables which together make up, or specify part of, an economic model are most clearly expressed in mathematical terms. In principle, this should permit empirical verification of the validity of the model through comparison of the model results against real outcomes. Clearly, though, this process only 'works' if a) the values of the factors being used are empirically realistic and b) they can be measured reliably and accurately.

9. As the economists Robert Shiller and George Akerlof confess: 'There are no standard ways to quantify the psychology of people'. Shiller and Akerlof, Animal Spirits.

10. In November, 2017, Barron's carried a lengthy article discussing the frank public admission by Janet Yellen, former Chair of the Fed, of the Fed's uncertainty as to the reason for the persistently low level of inflation in the US economy.

11. It is worth reading at length the comments of Steve Keen to realize how devastating this problem is for the 'scientific' claims of macroeconomic management.

'Lessons for Economics:

a) a system with unstable equilibria doesn't have to 'break down'. Instead the system displays complex cyclical behavior.

b) if equilibria are unstable neither the initial nor the final position of the model will be equilibrium positions.

c) extrapolating to the real world, actual economic variables are likely to be always in disequilibrium.

d) even as simple a system as one with 3 variables and 3 constants will display extremely complex dynamics with no stable equilibrium end-state.'

Steve Keen, Debunking Economics.

12. Considering only the last half century, the Fed created the Credit Crunch of 1966, the Credit Crunch of 1969 and then the massively destructive Great Inflation of the 1970s, which led directly to the financial crises of the 1980s. After the 1990s, which included the dotcom bubble, the Fed announced with pride in the 2000s that it was presiding over the Great Moderation, which instead turned out to be the Great Leveraging. After the collapse of the dotcom bubble, the Fed decided to engineer a 'wealth effect' by promoting a housing boom, which turned into the Great Housing Bubble. The Fed utterly failed to foresee the 2008 Crisis and to forecast the ensuing deep recession.

13. See Chapter 9, Blinded by Non-Science, for comments on 'statistical significance'.

14. He does issue the caveat that statistical correlation does not prove causation but the only element missing is an economic explanation and, when it comes to the vast range of potential economic explanations, a conveniently appropriate one is not hard to come by.

15. https://www.project-syndicate.org/commentary/
economics-must-change-in-three-ways-by-edmund-s-phelps-2019-01.

16. https://foreignpolicy.com/gt-essay/the-end-of-economics-fareed-zakaria/.

Chapter 7

THEORIES, MODELS AND ORTHODOXIES

'Economists, by and large, do not study the workings of the actual economic system. They theorize about it.' **Ronald Coase**.

'Practical men, who believe themselves to be quite exempt from any intellectual influence, are usually the slaves of some defunct economist. Madmen in authority, who hear voices in the air, are distilling their frenzy from some academic scribbler of a few years back.' **John Maynard Keynes**.

'In 2008 all of our models failed - all, across the board.' **Alan Greenspan**, former Chairman, Federal Reserve Bank of the USA, on CNBC, October 7th, 2011.

PART 1: THEORIES

The job of economists, obviously, is to develop interpretations and theories of economic behavior which successfully explain the way economies and their participants operate and to derive from their analysis policy recommendations for governments which will deliver stronger economic growth, subdued inflation and the avoidance of recessions. Macroeconomics - the study of the interaction between the major economic factors (growth, investment, consumption, employment, inflation etc.) in a whole, complex, developed economy - aims to describe and explain how these variables interconnect. Since the major economic factors are all interdependent, macroeconomic theories, if they are to qualify as reliably valid and useful, need to be comprehensive, universal and time-independent; they need to have the characteristics of economic Theories of Everything. The history of macroeconomics is the story of the rise and subsequent reassessment, and most often it seems significant discrediting, of a shifting succession of these macro theories about how whole economies work.

J. M. Keynes' great work **'The General Theory of Employment, Interest and Money'**, regarded as the first work of modern macro-economics, was published in 1936. Keynes integrated into a comprehensive general theory the many economic factors making up a whole economy (savings, investment, consumption, capital, money, employment etc.). Before Keynes these had tended to be the subject of separate or limited attention. The significant difference between his work and the less complete description and analysis of earlier economists, even the work of great figures like **Marshall**, is that it was comprehensive, incorporating the many major economic factors into a coherent whole. This comprehensiveness made it persuasive and led to its acceptance as the basis for major public policy measures.

Leading figures in economic history have contributed their own theories and interpretations of economic behavior and causation. Some focused on what can be termed, following **Keynes**, a comprehensive general theory of Economics; others have extended the scope of economic analysis and theory, focusing in greater detail on more specific and subsidiary aspects of economic behavior and activity (international trade, money, inflation, utility distribution, etc.). Adequate descriptions of their contributions can be found on the web, e.g. in their respective Wikipedia entries.

Historically, the development of economic thought has followed parallel, but conceptually different, paths. The first has been from the specific to the general, as the various theories emerging from the cumulative body of economic explanations have been synthesized into theories of the behavior of whole economies - macroeconomics. The second, conversely, is the path from generalization to increasing specificity, as broad theories have been supplanted or amplified by a narrower focus on particular aspects of economic behavior.

Theories and Crises

Since the inception of modern macroeconomics (generally accepted as dating from the publication of Keynes' 'General Theory'), the most useful and illuminating theories seem to have emerged as responses to severe economic crises or, in some cases, as reactions to policy mistakes. Keynes was inspired to write his General Theory by the widespread human misery of the Great Depression, considered to have been not caused, perhaps, but certainly prolonged and made very much worse by the restrictive monetary policy pursued by **Andrew Mellon**, the then U.S. Treasury Secretary. Mellon, a cold-turkey 'austerian' before his time, wished to 'purge the rottenness out of the system by liquidating labor, liquidating stocks, liquidating the farmers and liquidating real estate'. This is pretty much what happened, at enormous human cost, in the prolonged misery of the Great Depression. It was also what would have happened in the Crisis of 2008 had the economic authorities in the USA and elsewhere not taken drastic steps to prevent it.

At the global level, both the IMF and the Eurozone authorities have more recently borrowed amply from the Mellon playbook in the harsh policies they have imposed, in the name of macroeconomic orthodoxy, on emerging market economies and the Eurozone economy respectively. The cold-turkey austerity remedy for speculative financial bubbles such as triggered the Crisis of 2008 is also favored by the Austrian school of economics, following the unqualified libertarianism advocated by **Ludwig von Mises**.

Keynes took a different view. He believed that if private consumption collapsed then the government must fill the gap by undertaking and promoting public expenditure to stimulate a recovery, if necessary going into debt and incurring fiscal deficits, until animal spirits and confidence returned and a natural recovery process kicked in. Later, **Milton Friedman**'s work on monetary theory was a professional and intellectual response to the catastrophic inflation of the 1970s. It was their relevance to contemporary economic and social problems that led to the wide acceptance of these theories in the field of public policy.

Change and Decay: the Life-Cycle of Macroeconomic Theories

Thus the major developments in macroeconomic theory have tended to have their origins in the search for solutions to severe contemporary economic problems. It also seems that economic events, or human reactions to policies based on them, in due course disprove these new theories or show them to be irrelevant, often quite rapidly. Milton Friedman's belief in the strong causal link between the money supply and inflation has been, if not entirely disproven, certainly badly discredited by the persistent low inflation since the Crisis, in spite of enormous monetary expansion in the major developed economies. Similarly the Phillips curve theory of the inverse link between unemployment and inflation has also lost credibility as unemployment has tumbled to historical lows in spite of low inflation. Thus the life cycle of even major macroeconomic theories seems in practice to have a natural limit, as changes in events, or human reactions to the policies generated by the theories, render them ineffective.[1, 2]

Over the last 70 years the strong growth and spread of Economics has led to the development of a proliferation of major macroeconomic theories. These theories differ significantly and each has its devotees in Academia, in the financial world and in the media commentariat. (Chapter 8, 'Multiple Economic Universes and Theories of Everything', summarizes the conflicting theories.) Many of these macro theories are directly contradictory, reflecting disagreement among economists about the basic structure and operation of economies. This lack of agreement on the fundamental issues of macroeconomics is a serious problem for the status and usefulness of Economics. If economists can disagree so categorically about the fundamentals of how economies work it is very difficult to have much confidence in the validity of their theories.

The Macroeconomic Elite: What are your Qualifications?

However, if there is disagreement about the consequences and validity of their theories, professional macroeconomists are unanimous in insisting that new would-be candidates of their select corps jump through certain specific intellectual hoops if they are to be accepted as genuine members of the elite macroeconomist fraternity.

As **Dani Rodrik**, Professor of International Political Economy at the John F. Kennedy School of Government at Harvard, puts it: 'To be counted as an insider, as someone whose work should be taken seriously, you have to operate within the rules. The rules [demonstrate that I] have disciplined my research and have ensured that I know what I'm talking about. ....
Critics are not taken seriously - what is your model? - unless they're willing to follow the rules of engagement. Only card-carrying members of the profession are viewed as legitimate participants in economic debates - hence the paradox that economics is highly sensitive to criticism from inside, but extremely insensitive to criticism from outside [the profession].'

Rodrik is referring to two principal methodological processes: the use of models to express macroeconomic theories and the use of statistics. The serious shortcomings of economists' use of statistics are described in Chapter 9.

PART 2: MODELS

'Models .... make Economics a science. Selecting the right model is the key.' **Dani Rodrik, Economics Rules: the Use and Misuse of Economic Ideas,** 2015.

'Nothing in these abstract economic models actually works in the real world. It doesn't matter how many footnotes they put in, or how many ways they tinker around the edges. The whole enterprise is totally rotten at the core: it has no relation to reality.' **Noam Chomsky.**

'I cannot see how the practice of modelling can have scientific value unless models can provide genuine explanations of the real world.' **Robert Sugden,** 2013, quoted by **Lawrence Boland, Model Building in Economics,** 2014.

'Even when a truly deductive, hypothesis-testing approach is followed, much of what economists produce is not really testable in any strict sense of the word. The field is rife with models that yield contradictory conclusions. ..... The profession's progression of favored models tends to follow fad and fashion.' **D. Rodrik,** ibid.

'The only question of interest is whether economists and econometricians can build models that are useful rather than mathematically elegant'. **Lawrence Boland, Model Building in Economics,** 2014.

'Any assurance economists pretend to with regards to cause and effect (in models) is merely a pose or an illusion.' **Emanuel Derman, Models Behaving Badly,** 2011.

As noted, the early fathers of Economics, **Adam Smith** and **John Stuart Mill,** expressed their theories of the workings of economies in plain prose. In the second half of the 19th century economists began to express their theories of economic behavior and relationships and of the operation of whole economies using mathematics. The French economist **Leon Walras**, besides using mathematics to express economic relationships, started using calculus to generate economic models incorporating multiple economic factors (See Chapter 6, Notes).

In the mid-1930s, the American economist Wassily Leontief began to develop large scale economic models. Later, in the 1950s and 1960s as economic data became more available, econometricians began to develop very large models. 'Very large' in this case meant models with a very large number of equations.[3] Since then model-building, greatly boosted by the explosion in computer power since the 1960s, has been the method of choice for professional economists seeking to express their theories of how economies work. The growing scope and quality of the statistics produced by national economics bodies, providing more and better data for the theorist to work with, greatly assisted this process. In parallel with this development the rapid and easy analytical capabilities made available through the computing revolution spurred the production of an exploding proliferation of theoretical economic models.[4]

The present dominant standing of economic models in the methods of professional economists is thoroughly described, and strongly defended, by **Dani Rodrik** in his book, **Economics Rules: the Rights and Wrongs of the Dismal Science**. According to him, training in Economics consists essentially in learning a sequence of models. **Rodrik's** book reads as a propaganda exercise in favor of economic models and in support of their claim to be useful and realistic. He defends economic models as 'capturing the most relevant aspect of reality in a given context' and as 'essential to understanding the workings of society'. 'What makes a model useful', he says, 'is that it captures an aspect of reality.' Perhaps as a result of this trend, the creation of new economic models has become the required path to advancement in the Economics profession.

Rodrik maintains that the multiplicity of current macroeconomic models and theories, many of them directly contradictory, are all useful since they offer explanations of, and solutions for, a wide variety of economic situations and problems. Choose your economic explanation to fit your circumstances and requirements, he proposes. According to Rodrik, all the numerous current theories of fundamental human economic behavior have value and use in certain circumstances. Taken together, he maintains, these models and theories constitute a growing body of useful advances in economic management. The Economics profession should take comfort from this and disregard the imputations of social uselessness being bandied about.

Yet, as he also admits, 'the field is rife with models that yield contradictory conclusions,' and furthermore, 'the [Economics] profession's progression of favored models tends to follow fad and fashion.' If the validity of models turns on shifting fashionability, Economics has decidedly lost touch with reality.

Models: the Horizontal Advance

'My point about economics is different. It is that economics as a science advances 'horizontally' (by multiplying models) rather than 'vertically' (by newer ones replacing older ones). Economics advances also by better methods of model selection.' **Dani Rodrik, Economics Rules.**

Dani Rodrik proposes that the appropriate way to judge the wider scientific usefulness of Economics is to see it as advancing 'horizontally', with every new model or theory adding to the sum of certain knowledge, rather than, as in the natural sciences, 'vertically', where new, more accurate theories systematically replace older, discredited ones.

Thus the so-called 'hard' sciences advance by defining progressively more accurate descriptions of the real world. Theories are proposed and are tested rigorously against factual reality. The confirmation may take a considerable time - witness the recent discovery of the gravitation waves predicted by Einstein's Theory of Relativity early last century or, as noted earlier, the decades-long gap between the prediction of the **Higgs** boson in 1964 and the confirmation of its existence in 2012. Using Rodrik's parlance, in the natural sciences human knowledge advances 'vertically', entering higher, more accurate and superior territory with each confirmed theory and discovery. The confirmation of a new, more accurate descriptive theory consigns the earlier, inaccurate and disproven theory to the dustbin of history.

No such claim can be made for Economics. The problem is that economic behavior, whether of the individual, the firm or the whole economy, changes continuously: it is simply too infinitely variable to act as the basis for any valid prediction or model.[5]

Nonetheless, in support of his claim that Economics is not only useful but that it is also a science, **Rodrik** proposes that each new economic model (provided of course that it is proposed by a 'card-carrying' member of the profession (his words)) does validly advance our knowledge of the world. As noted, for him the multiplicity of economic models and explanations, many of them contradictory, constitute a 'horizontal' advance in knowledge.[6]

Yet, according to Rodrik, as he is honest enough to admit, the usefulness of an economic model for the management of a given set of conditions depends fundamentally on human judgment - the model does not stand by itself and cannot be relied on without human intervention. If this is so any economic model's value is both inherently uncertain and crucially dependent on the exercise of human judgment in its application. This is really to admit that the practice of Economics is as variable, uncertain and unpredictable as baking a complicated cake with questionable ingredients in a dodgy oven; predictable it ain't.

Model Fallacies

There are additional flaws in **Rodrik**'s defence of economic models. To apply the term 'model' to an economic analysis or theory is to claim that it is more than just an organized, accurate explanation of a one-off, specific situation. It is to claim that the analysis in question has in some measure wider validity: it can be reliably applied to other similar situations.

The examples of the use of models which **Rodrik** gives from his work in developing economies seem not much more than the application of elementary, business-like, common-sense thinking to solve a problem. It seems frankly pretentious, by describing the result of this process as a model, to elevate it to the exercise of a complex and arcane professional talent available only to academic economists.

If a model, particularly a macroeconomic model, is to act as a reliably useful description of an economic process and perhaps serve as the basis for a policy initiative, it must be to some extent universal. It must hold good for more than a single situation, more than a short period and for more than a small group of economic agents, whether consumers, investors or businessmen. The problem is, as Keynes was continuously aware, that economic behavior is inherently too variable to permit the formulation of valid economic models.

An additional problem is that, as noted above, human judgment is always required in selecting and adapting a model to any economic problem. If so, the implication of wider (or at least more than limited, one-off) validity implied by the use of the word model to describe the process is negated if every model must be tweaked and altered by human judgment to fit the unique, particular circumstances of each application.

In fact, economists are in the difficult contradictory position of seeking respect as purveyors of scientifically-based expertise while at the same time needing to apply over-riding human judgment in recommending policy moves.

Econs and Modls

The spreading use of models and abstract mathematics in Economics was apparent enough more than 40 years ago to encourage **Axel Leijonhuvfud**, an economist then at the University of California, to write a spoof quasi-anthropological paper on the 'tribe' of Econs, **'Life among the Econs'**, published in the Western Economic Journal September, 1973.[7]

'Worse than Useless': Large-scale Macroeconomic Models

'Efforts to construct large-scale economic models have been singularly unproductive to date. In fact they have often led us astray.' **Dani Rodrik**, ibid.

'We simply do not have a settled successful theory of the macroeconomy.' **N. Kocherlakota**, past President of the Minneapolis Federal Reserve, July 16th, 2016.

Most of the large-scale models produced by the various theoretical economic sects have little or no significant basis in, or attachment to, the real world. Even leaving aside the 2008 Crisis, the record is that, as tools for forecasting and for the formulation of realistic policy measures, large-scale economic models have turned out to be pretty well useless, not to say dangerously misleading. Furthermore, they suffer from the severe methodological drawbacks outlined in Chapter 6 (reductive simplification and selection of data, indeterminacy of dynamic multi-factor equations, the questionable significance of statistical projections of factor values from past data, etc.).

No Model, No Career

In spite of the many severe flaws described above, the creation of economic models to express theories of how economies work has become the required method of explanation within the Economics profession. More importantly, the consequence of this intellectual tribalism has been that model-making has become the required path to advancement in the profession. As **Rodrik** puts it: 'If you have no model, you're not taken seriously'. Rather like **Gregory Mankiw**'s insistence on the indispensability of mathematics, the Economics profession insists on a commitment to, and proficiency in, model-making as a necessary condition of acceptance into the economic elite.

PART 3: ORTHODOXIES

'Orthodoxy means not thinking - not needing to think.' **George Orwell, 1984.**

If macroeconomic theories are successful (i.e. they provided at the time a persuasive explanation of the critical events in question and feasible recommendations for solving the problem) and if they are proposed by forceful personalities, they gain the status of orthodoxies. An attractive new theory is taken up in Academia; Economics departments in the universities start to teach it. Textbooks for university Economics students are written to disseminate, embellish and promote it and soon generations of students are brought up to accept the latest theory as pretty well unquestioned orthodoxy.

This ready attribution of orthodoxy is dangerous, both intellectually and socially. As **Keynes** was well aware, and never forgot, the essential and defining feature of economic behavior, whether at the level of the individual or the firm, or at the macro level of an entire economy, is that the many agents in a complex developed economy are continuously altering and adapting their economic reactions and behavior to the myriad shifts and pressures not only of events but also of psychology and human emotions. Often they do so in contradictory ways and often it seems in ways that are very different from their reactions to earlier episodes of the same or similar conditions.

Global Orthodoxy: the IMF

It is not only national governments who have adopted and persistently stuck to questionable macroeconomic orthodoxies. The **International Monetary Fund** (IMF) was set up by the major powers to coordinate action to assist economic recovery after World War II. The Bretton Woods system, within which it operated, had been established by the major powers in July, 1944, to create a global monetary structure for the relationships between currencies. In the Bretton Woods system currencies were tied indirectly, via their link to the US$, to Gold. Bretton Woods collapsed when Nixon cut the link of the US$ to gold in 1971. Thereafter the IMF assumed a new role as guarantor of global currency stability, acting as lender-of-last-resort to countries in 'temporary' balance-of-payments difficulties.

In the early 1980s several Latin American countries got seriously into debt. They had borrowed large sums from willing international banks in the 1970s at interest rates which were then low, relying on continued global growth to see them through. The borrowings were denominated in US$. When recession struck and their economies tanked the financial effect was devastating. Dollar interest rates rose strongly. As a result the currencies of many developing countries (the Mexican peso in 1982, the Thai baht, South Korean won and Indonesian rupiah in the late 1990s, to name only a few) collapsed, making their foreign debt even more burdensome and pushing these countries into financial crisis. The IMF coordinated bail-outs for these economies, providing loans to enable them to ride out what was viewed as a severe but temporary problem and avoid the repercussions of full default.

Naturally the IMF insisted on conditions for its help. These conditions were that the countries it helped must adopt cold-turkey austerity measures. The essence of these measures was the imposition of its preferred economic orthodoxy - hard-nosed, classical, free-market capitalism with balanced budgets, privatization and the elimination of price controls and government subsidies, including social market payments to the poor. Following its preferred macroeconomic model, the IMF in effect aimed to transform Latin America's countries abruptly into capitalist, free-trade economies. The consequences of its hard-nosed insistence on its preferred orthodoxy were a collapse in the growth rates of these countries, massive increases in unemployment and a severe drop in living standards, with a widespread increase in poverty for large numbers of people. The experience ruined the reputation of the IMF in its wards for a generation.

Recent economic history shows that while some adopted theories have attained considerable durability most have only a short meteoric lifespan as orthodoxies. The current and still dominant macroeconomic theory, the so-called Dynamic Stochastic General Equilibrium model, which was in large part responsible for the Crisis of 2008 (see below), has, unfortunately, enjoyed a long ascendancy.

Fifteen Minutes of Fame

- **The Phillips Curve**

An example of the transitory and unstable character of economic orthodoxies is the history of the Phillips Curve. The severe inflation in the major global economies in the 1970s drew the attention of economists to this theory, first propounded in 1958 by **William Phillips**, then a professor of Economics at the LSE in London. Phillips posited an inverse relationship between the rate of unemployment and the rate of inflation, the latter rising as the former fell below a certain level (judged at the time in the UK to be 6%). The notion of NAIRU, the non-accelerating inflation rate of unemployment, figured for quite a while in the comments and thinking of economists and their political masters.

Consequently, the theory, which did indeed appear to be an accurate and useful interpretation of the behavior of the UK and other economies during the inflationary 1970s, gained the status of unquestioned orthodoxy, both in Economics and in government. But the collapse of inflation during the Great Moderation after 1982, accompanied by falling unemployment, discredited the theory. The Crisis of 2008 was followed by the Great Recession; in the developed economies inflation has continued to remain well below historical levels even while unemployment rates have fallen, in many cases to historical lows. The Phillips Curve has accordingly been discredited and no longer enjoys orthodoxy status. Its changing status illustrates well the essentially variable and contingent nature of even persuasive macroeconomic theories.

- **Monetarist Theory and Inflation**

The experience of the major economies since the Crisis also strongly confirms the transitory validity of even major macroeconomic theories. The persistently low level of inflation in the US economy, hovering for long near the brink of deflation, has torpedoed the status, as a durably reliable law of economic behavior, of the **Friedman/Chicago** school monetary theory. The US Federal Reserve balance sheet has ballooned to more than $6 trillion, as the bank has boosted the money supply over the last 12 years in an attempt to kick-start the US economy, yet inflation is still conspicuous by its absence and, for the Fed, is still a major conundrum. This measure has failed in its assumed purpose and left the money-supply/inflation theory in disarray.

- **Deficit Spending**

At present it seems that the only major tenet of macroeconomic theory to withstand the test of time is the Keynesian proposal for increasing public spending to offset recessions arising from deficient private sector demand and the arguments for this have much more to do with social policy than pure economic theory. (In a diametrically opposite view, the **Mises Institute** continues to propose the application of severe austerity measures, à la Mellon, to solve the depressive effects of the boom/bust aftermath of the 2008 Crisis.)

Over time the Keynesian policy response adopted by the Roosevelt administration (with the great additional impetus of the public expenditure of the Second World War) acquired the status of an orthodoxy. It is still accepted almost universally as one of the fundamental pillars of macroeconomic management.[8] In 1960 J.F. Kennedy's response to the recession of that year was to embrace deficit spending.[9]

In the USA, as a response to the Crisis of 2008, Ben Bernanke, and later Janet Yellen, vigorously pursued a neo-classical monetary policy, aggressively expanding the Fed balance sheet. The result has been a major artificial bubble in asset prices, unprecedented distortion in the credit and debt markets and penal consequences in the savings and pensions markets. Advocates of this approach such as Paul Krugman and Joseph Stiglitz regularly applaud this policy in the media.[10]

• **Cold-Turkey Austerity**

Recently the **Eurozone** has been the theater for another demonstration of the dangers of clinging inflexibly to an orthodoxy. Many of the southern Eurozone countries (Portugal, Italy, Greece, and Spain, with France in much the same position) remain, more than 10 years after the Crisis and after huge monetary stimulus by the ECB, in difficult economic and social straits. Yet the European Commission and the ECB have continued to impose a regime of strict austerity on these weaker Eurozone members (except of course France, which has yet again received a free pass in spite of a debt-to-GDP ratio near 100%, persistent low growth at less than 2% p.a. and systemic fiscal deficits which regularly exceed the specified 3% Eurozone maximum).

This insistence on continued austerity comes in spite of the fact that the so-called PIGS economies (Portugal, Italy, Greece and Spain) continue to suffer from little growth, unemployment around 20% (and youth unemployment around 50%), public debt levels equal to (or, in Italy, well above) the size of their economies and no prospect of lasting recovery while they remain members of the Eurozone. There are no signs that the regime of continued severe austerity imposed by the European Commission and the ECB is generating in any of these countries a recovery which will be strong and durable enough to free them from their debt bondage. They face continued misery and increasing social unrest.[11,12]

In the past, before they adopted the Euro, these countries would devalue from time to time, restoring their competitiveness and enabling a slow adaptation to competitive conditions and the resumption of normal life. Now, Germany, in the Eurozone policy driving seat and playing the role of financial disciplinarian, is insisting on hair-shirt austerity orthodoxy, requiring these countries to 'put their economic house in order'. In effect these countries are supposed to wave a magic, all-potent social wand and, hey presto! morph into mini-Germanys. (Germany steadfastly and conveniently ignores the fact that their own economic and social reforms in the first decade of this century had the immense cushion and support of a euro exchange rate much weaker than its own Deutsch Mark would have had.) The result is severe and persistent social distress, with no end in sight. It also constitutes a deeply irresponsible and hypocritical, not to say cynical, pretence that everything will work out OK in the end and that the structure of the Euro is not fatally flawed.

Both within the Economics profession and in politics, therefore, the regular process seems to be that theories which have been successful in explaining and curing specific economic crises are uncritically accepted as reliably valid for the future. There are two significant and regrettable political consequences of this. Politicians, with their continuous need for apparently expert justification for their economic policies, are happy to go along with this essentially inertial process. Secondly, in turn, the public, even less able to judge the real merits of a complicated economic model or theory, are happy to accept that their elected representatives have duly examined and scrutinized the professional economic thinking behind the policy proposals.

The cultural and social process of orthodoxy-creation in Economics is of course, greatly assisted by the opacity, even to the intelligent man in the street, of the dense mathematics in which economic theories and models are now expressed (see Chapter 6). As noted, the opaque mathematics in which economists express their theories effectively insulates them from wide critical examination.

PART 4: DSGE: ONE ORTHODOXY TO RULE THEM ALL!

For most of the period since the Second World War the dominant macroeconomic model followed by most of the world's central banks and finance ministries to define the framework and operating mechanics of the economies they are responsible for managing has been the so-called Dynamic Stochastic General Equilibrium model (DSGE). It still is.[13]

This model lay behind the policy pursued by the Fed in its management of the US economy in the years before the Crisis. It was the unwavering confidence of the Fed, and in particular of **Alan Greenspan**, its Chairman, in the reliability of the DSGE macroeconomic model which was one of the two key factors responsible for the Fed's failure to foresee the Crisis and take steps to prevent it (the other was his and the Fed's belief in unrestrained free markets and deregulation).

The choice of macroeconomic models and their development and refinement within central banks and Treasuries is fully the responsibility of the institution's professional economic staff. At present, according to its website, the Fed employs more than 300 Economics PhDs plus a large number of junior and supporting staff. These staff numbers are matched in the rest of the US Federal Reserve System. Achieving a reliable model of how the economy works is not only the major focus of the research effort of the Fed's economic staff but also, since the adopted models generate the policies they recommend, the most important influence on their policy advice. The individuals in charge of these institutions and their staff are accordingly responsible for the consequences of the policies their models generate and which they recommend.

The DSGE Model: the Articles of Faith

The DSGE model relies on two principal tenets and a few secondary ones. The major tenets are:

- economic systems have an inherent, automatic tendency to return to equilibrium from any imbalance, if not interfered with, and

- human beings behave with perfect rational self-interest when making economic choices.

The secondary tenets are:

- it is legitimate to take the behavior of one abstract individual as representative of the behavior of an entire class of economic agents (such as consumers or businessmen) and conclusions derived from this extreme simplification are valid for the entire group,

- economic agents do not alter or adapt their behavior in response to policies or changing conditions,

- money, debt and financial flows are irrelevant to the workings of an economy and can safely be ignored.

For a detailed and comprehensive description of the severe shortcomings of the DSGE model and its dominance of prevailing macroeconomic orthodox thinking, **Steve Keen**'s book, **Debunking Economics**, cannot be improved on.[14]

A recent paper by **Joseph Stiglitz** in the series of Working Papers published by the National Bureau of Economic Research also provides a thorough critique of the failings of the DSGE model.[15]

The DSGE Model: Fallacies

i) Equilibrium: 'Leave them alone and they'll come home'

'Equilibrium is blither.' **J. M. Keynes**.

'If you hear a "prominent" economist using the word 'equilibrium,' or 'normal distribution,' do not argue with him; just ignore him, or try to put a rat down his shirt.' **Nassim Nicholas Taleb, The Bed of Procrustes: Philosophical and Practical Aphorisms.**

'A perfect example of blackboard economics - clearly and even scandalously unrepresentative of any recognizable economic system.' **Ronald Coase**, commenting on general equilibrium theory.

The most serious error of the DSGE model is its fundamental belief in the natural equilibrium state of economies. The belief that the normal state of economies is one of natural equilibrium, where the various impulses of demand, supply, investment and savings etc. are automatically balanced, had its origins in **Adam Smith**'s 'Wealth of Nations'. Smith's description of the 'invisible hand', through the operation of which the conflicting interests of the consumer and the producer, the entrepreneur and the investor, were naturally, automatically and continuously, reconciled through the price mechanism, provided a persuasive and seemingly accurate description of the workings of a complex economy. A significant feature of this interpretation was that the balancing process happened without the intervention of any external influence: the desirable equilibrium was achieved though the free, unrestricted operation of the market.

As a result this idea held, and still holds, particular attraction for economists who believe for social and political reasons in the superior value of free and unregulated markets. The theory was and is psychologically seductive. It delivered a seemingly desirable end state - economic equilibrium - which is achieved automatically by the natural operation of the market without the need for any external intervention. Later, leading economists, like the French economist Leon Walras (who married the abstract principle described by Adam Smith to the use of mathematics), and Alfred Marshall in the UK, adopted it readily and crafted the use of mathematics and the development of economic models round it.

Since then the 'steady state', natural equilibrium theory has assumed the status of an unquestioned orthodoxy. The large Economics departments of central banks and finance ministries, peopled with professional economists who have attained high post-graduate academic status in their subject, have for long been uncritical believers in the 'natural equilibrium' theory.[16]

Unfortunately, as an accurate, reliable theory providing useful guidance for effective economic policy in the management of a developed economy, the DSGE theory has proven not only useless but positively dangerous. It was their uncritical belief in an unregulated automatic and natural return to equilibrium that was the chief reason for the disastrous failure of the US authorities to take steps to control and limit the explosion in credit which led to the Crisis of 2008. In fact, as Alan Greenspan admitted in 2011, when the Crisis struck, every single one of the Fed's macroeconomic models failed.

ii) Where's the money?

'...if you look at mainstream economics there are three things you will not find in a mainstream economic model - Banks, Debt, and Money. How anybody can think they can analyze capital while leaving out Banks, Debt, and Money is to me a bit like an ornithologist trying to work out how a bird flies whilst ignoring that the bird has wings...' **Steve Keen, Debunking Economics.**

'More than 5 years since the outbreak of the credit crunch most economic models still have no financial component.' **John Plender, _Financial Times_,** January 13th, 2013.

Besides its persistent misguided faith in equilibrium as the natural, stable state of economies, achieved automatically through the free play of frictionless markets, the DSGE model has another critical and extraordinary flaw: it utterly ignores the role played in a developed economy by credit and finance. This omission seems so fundamental and glaring a defect that it is difficult to believe, yet it is nonetheless true. DSGE theories treat money as a residual factor in economies; they ignore entirely the crucial fact that the principal influence on the level of activity in an economy is changes in the supply and/or cost of credit.

It is changes in the availability and cost of credit from the banking system that have the strongest and most direct impact on the level of business, investment and consumer demand. Until the prolonged slowdown which has prevailed since the 2008 Crisis, a change in the terms of credit availability was the chief policy tool used by central banks to control the effects of business cycles and manage the economy. Yet the DSGE model has nothing to say on the question of credit; on this key issue it is silent (or perhaps, more accurately, dumb).

Hyman Minsky and Financial Instability

Yet these major macroeconomic flaws in the DSGE model (the belief in natural, unregulated equilibrium and the failure to take account of the major role of credit) had been identified and addressed by some macroeconomists well before they led to the Crisis of 2008. The economist **Hyman Minsky** believed that capitalist economies tended naturally, not towards equilibrium, but towards its opposite – disequilibrium and instability.

Minsky's analysis of the business cycles and recessions which the US economy had experienced regularly over many decades led him to the conclusion that a macroeconomic theory like DSGE, which by definition could not experience recessions, was very seriously faulty. As early as 1982 he published a collection of essays with the title 'Can "It" Happen Again'. The 'It' he was referring to was the Great Depression. The subtitle of the book was 'Essays on Instability and Finance'. For Minsky 'a fundamental characteristic of our economy is that the financial system swings between robustness and fragility and these swings are an integral part of the process that generates business cycles'.

In a later book 'Stabilizing an Unstable Economy', originally published in 1986, Minsky set out his views at greater length. Minsky died in 1996 but his book was re-issued in 2008 following the Crisis. As Henry Kaufman, the former partner in Salomon Brothers, wrote in his foreword to the 2008 edition, 'If Minsky were alive today, he could justly claim "I told you so".'

In spite of the accuracy and relevance of his analysis Minsky was uniformly ignored during his life, not only within the Economics departments of central banks and finance ministries but within the Economics profession as a whole. The reason for this profession-wide disregard was that Minsky's instability theory seriously questioned the validity of the major pillar of the DSGE model: natural equilibrium. His theory was therefore a challenge to the prevailing order. It was heresy and accordingly it received the sort of treatment that religious heresies typically received in medieval times: brutal suppression.[17]

The Fed and the DSGE model: Systematic Suppression of Dissent

Yet there was another reason for the systematic disregard of Minsky within the Economics profession. This was that for many decades now the Federal Reserve has held such a dominant role within the Economics profession that it has been able to exert overwhelming pressure to discourage and discredit attempts to question or criticize its preferred macroeconomic model.

The last decades have seen the birth of a large number of alternative fundamental macroeconomic theories and many of these have become schools of thought within Economics (see Chapter 8). These theories have sprung from different analytical approaches and have generated a range of different, and often contradictory, policy themes and preferences. They have included some theories of the structure of whole economies, such as the Minsky model, which were much more complete and much more realistic.

It would be natural to expect that the Federal Reserve, with its primary responsibility for the management of the US economy and the vast professional resources it enjoys, would have devoted serious manpower and effort to fully investigating the merits of alternative macroeconomic strategies. The fact is that, so far from keeping an open mind as to the potential usefulness of alternative theories of macroeconomic management, the Fed has over several decades systematically sought to discourage any challenges to its favored DSGE macroeconomic model.

A recent article in the **Huffington Post** (HP), 'How the Federal Reserve Bought the Economics Profession', spells out the results of an investigation by the HP into what is on the face of it the wholesale suborning of the Economics profession by the Federal Reserve over the last three decades.[18]

The opening paragraph of the article summarizes the main result of HP's investigation: 'The Federal Reserve, through its extensive network of consultants, visiting scholars, alumni and staff economists, so thoroughly dominates the field of economics that real criticism of the central bank has become a career liability for members of the profession.' The article provides extensive chapter-and-verse examples of the Fed's hammer-lock control of the profession over the three decades before 2008.[19]

The consequence has been a long-standing, profession-wide suppression of criticism of the Fed's preferred DSGE model. This model had become macroeconomic orthodoxy; it was not to be questioned. It is therefore no surprise that the model's great deficiencies received no serious public consideration and discussion in the decades before the 2008 Crisis. The quotation from **George Orwell** at the head of Part 3 of this chapter comes, appropriately, from his book '1984'.

This institutional imposition of a disastrous orthodoxy was in large part responsible for the failure of the Fed, in the persons of **Alan Greenspan** and **Ben Bernanke**, together with **Lawrence Summers** at the US Treasury, to foresee the Crisis.

The DSGE Model Fails - Big Time

As noted earlier, a summary of the macroeconomic events in the US economy over the last few decades might run as follows:

'Considering only the last half century, the Fed created the Credit Crunch of 1966, the Credit Crunch of 1969 and then the massively destructive Great Inflation of the 1970s, which led directly to the financial crises of the 1980s. The 1990s included the dotcom bubble. In the 2000s the Fed announced with pride that it was presiding over the Great Moderation, which turned out to be the Great Leveraging. After the collapse of the dotcom market, the Fed decided to promote a 'wealth effect' by promoting a housing boom, which turned into the Great Housing Bubble. The Fed utterly failed to foresee the 2008 Crisis which ensued and to forecast the resulting deep recession.'

The Crisis brutally exposed the invalidity of the dominant macroeconomic model used by the Federal Reserve and the US Treasury in formulating the economic policy of the USA. This failure had disastrous consequences for the lives of many millions across the globe and, more than ten years after the Crisis, the world economy is still recovering.

But the failure was very much more fundamental. It was not simply a failure of bad execution and mismanagement; it was a failure of the very basis of the theory and practice of macroeconomics.

Chapter 7: Notes

1. In fact this process of decay and growing irrelevance has been recognized by economists for quite a while. Charles Goodhart, chief economist of the Bank of England at the time, propounded in 1975 a law (now named after him) which states that once a policy measure has become a target it ceases to be a good measure. In a related thesis, in a 1976 paper the Lucas Critique states that no sound predictions of the effects of a change in economic policy can be deduced from historical data.

2. An excellent recent book, 'The Economists' Hour' by **Binyamin Appelbaum** describes fully the history of the adoption and application of the major macroeconomic policy theories since the emergence of Economics after World War II.

3. For example, the number of equations in a typical model increased from 25 in the 1950s to more than 400 in the 1960s and to more than 1,000 today. Daniel Little, writing in 1995, refers to economic models with several hundred equations, variables and parameters as 'medium-sized'.

4. It also generated a parallel explosion in the number of macroeconomic schools-of-thought, many of them contradictory. (See Chapter 8)

5. However, the new science of Behavioral Economics has discovered several patterns of human economic behavior. These developments are addressed in Chapter 9.

6. The notion of a horizontal advance would not, one imagines, make much sense to a military commander as a strategy for conquering new territory.

7. Leijonhufvud invented the term 'Econs' to describe the tribe of professional economists rather than the unnatural and unrealistic beings who populate economic models. Behind his use of the term is a sardonic disbelief in the unrealistic assumptions on which much of modern economic thinking is based. In Leijonhufvud's tribe the priestly 'Math-Econs' regard themselves as of distinctly higher caste than the 'Micros' or 'Macros'. There is considerable bad blood between the castes and little caste intermarriage. Econs despise the political science tribe (Polscis), the sociologists tribe (Sociogs) and even more the development economists (Devlops) who regularly make the mistake of breaking tribal taboos by associating with the other tribes. Apprentice Econs must earn their adult status and ultimately appointment to the rank of tribal elder by producing 'modls'.
   Leijonhufvud is a member of the Advisory Board of the newly-formed

Institute for New Economic Thinking (see Chapter 12).

Richard Thaler, in his recent book '**Misbehaving**', describing the origins and development of Behavioral Economics, suggests the term *homo economicus* or Econ for short. Thaler's *homo economicus* is a sub-species of *homo sapiens*, i.e. mankind. Econs live their lives in accordance with the abstract, mathematical theories and models of economic behavior which still dominate Economics. Thaler uses the term Humans for normal human beings like you and me. His point is that Econs are not really human and don't display the typical varied behavior of normal human beings when making most day-to-day, real-life economic decisions. Thaler has a lot of well-justified fun describing the utterly unrealistic behavior of Econs and their complete divorce from the real world and from the way actual human beings make economic decisions in real life.

8. It should be noted that one of the most persuasive arguments for Keynesian deficit spending to offset economic recession or depression is not economic but, simply and fundamentally, social and ethical: the relief of human distress. Keynes was very aware of this and his comments at the time show that it was this, quite as much as any consideration of theoretical Economics, which lay at the base of his concern and his policy recommendations.

9. In 2002 Dick Cheney, referring to the economic policies of the Reagan administration, declared that Reagan had 'proved that deficits don't matter'; Reagan oversaw a tripling of US government debt.

10. Since 1960, after the recovery from World War II, the US economy experienced a recurring succession of business cycles. The seemingly regular pattern was that growth and expansion led to higher inflation triggering a response in the form of a monetary squeeze through higher interest rates, leading to a fall in investment, then a fall in employment, a slowdown/recession and a moderation in inflation. Since the Crisis, however, this reliably predictable cycle seems to have been decisively broken. The cessation of the familiar cycle has made the monetary management task of the Federal Reserve much more difficult.

11. Recently we have seen the EU authorities congratulate themselves on Greece's exit from the financial intensive-care ward. The conditions of the rescue package make it clear that Greeks are expected to put up with a desperate, miserable existence for decades to come. By all accounts 500,000 of the best and brightest have already emigrated. This is a recipe for human and national catastrophe.

12. The economist **Yanis Varoufakis** led the negotiations for Greece. He has written two admirable and excellent books: one about the disastrous economic policies which the Eurozone has pursued and continues to pursue and the second about his in-the-trenches experience of representing Greece as the country's finance minister. The first book, '**And the Weak Suffer What They Must**', is a devastating criticism of the Eurozone authorities' blind adherence to irrational and disastrous economic dogma. The second, the remarkable '**Adults in the Room**', sets out even-handedly and in very thorough detail the entire sequence of the

discussions with the 'troika' (the IMF, the ECB and the European Commission) in the long-drawn out Greek bailout negotiations. His book records the dismaying and inflexible insistence of the 'troika' on imposing perpetual, socially-catastrophic austerity on Greece as the price for extending additional loans to a country already absurdly over its head in debt while pretending that this financing constituted a responsible positive response to Greece's plight. Rightly, Varoufakis calls this 'economic idiocy'. Another book, '**Welcome to the Poisoned Chalice: The Destruction of Greece and the Future of Europe**', by Varoufakis' friend and colleague, **James K. Galbraith**, confirms his reports.

Varoufakis also records, damningly, that the economic model used by the IMF in calculating the effects of the policies it was insisting on (which it refused to reconsider) was disastrously and elementarily unrealistic. In effect their position combined a double error: a commitment to disastrous and unrealistic policies based on a model incorporating large, critical and elementary errors.

13. In the model title the terms 'dynamic' and 'stochastic' indicate that the model is capable of adapting successfully to changing economic conditions. As the Crisis demonstrated this is simple nonsense.

14. See in particular Chapter 10 of his book: 'They didn't see it coming'.

15. **Joseph Stiglitz**, NBER, Working Paper 23795, September/November 2017, '**Where Modern Macroeconomics Went Wrong**'. Stiglitz' critique is comprehensive and authoritative. Stiglitz was Chairman of the Council of Economic Advisers in the Clinton administration and, in the course of his paper, reports (interestingly, in the light of the paper's main argument) that 'many of the considerations which we focused on are excluded from the standard models'. Bizarrely, in spite of demonstrating at length in the main body of his paper that the DSGE model is fatally unrealistic, he concludes his paper by presenting a new version of the DSGE model embellished with new bells and whistles, supposedly to remedy the model's failings. He presents no empirical evidence that his new model corresponds with what happens in the real world and it is very difficult to see this as anything more than another elaborate exercise in useless mathematical abstraction.

16. A more detailed description of how the notion of equilibrium gained its ascendancy on Economics is given by Steve Keen: Debunking Economics, pages 172 et seq.

17. Steve Keen, in his comments on Minsky, reports that only one paper by Minsky saw publication in a major economic journal, in the American Economic Review in 1957. His name appeared in another as discussant.

18. http://huffingtonpost.com/2009/09/07priceless-how-the-federal_n_278805. This article was first published in October, 2009 and updated in May, 2013.

19. According to the Huffington Post investigation, the Fed maintains its control of the US Economics world using various means. These include: control of academic Economics through contractual relationships with prominent academic

economists; dominant influence in many professional journals through contractual relationships with the editorial board members (e.g. the Journal of Monetary Economics where, in 2008, more than half of the editorial board members were then on the Fed payroll); the awarding of contracts to academic economists (the HP article reports that the Fed spent $389.2 million on this research in 2008 and comments that 'this is a lot of money' for a relatively small number of economists'). Again according to HP, besides these contractual financial inducements, being in the Fed's good books leads to other good stuff like invitations to Fed conferences and offers of visiting scholarships with the bank.

Chapter 8

———⚬⚬⚬———

MULTIPLE UNIVERSES, ECONOMICS T.O.E.

'Contrary to what most economists would have you believe there isn't just one kind of economics…...' **Ha-Joon Chang, Economics: the User's Guide**.

'Economics allows multiple interpretations of reality. While this is fatal to its pretensions to be considered as a science, it does give persistent oxygen to the survival and even flourishing of fundamentally contradictory macroeconomic theories: a warm bath of non-provability.' **Steve Keen, Debunking Economics**.

Since the major economic factors are all interdependent, macroeconomic theories aspire to be economic Theories of Everything - that is, to deliver an explanation of the mechanics and operation of economies which comprehensively includes all the factors making up a developed economy. Furthermore, if it is to deserve the title, an economic Theory of Everything must, like its elder brother in the 'hard sciences', be universally valid. It must hold true not just for one economy or for one period of time but for all economies in any period of time. In the hard science of cosmology, Theories of Everything aspire to deliver a comprehensive explanation of how the universe works and these theories are subject to proof or disproof by testing against the evidence of the real world.

In the same way, if Economics has a valid claim to be a 'hard' science on a par with chemistry or biology or other branches of science, its statements too must be universal and time-independent. In hard science there is only one reality; in accordance with the fundamental principle of valid scientific discovery, macroeconomic theories of how whole economies work must be testable, as Einstein's theory of relativity was, by the standard discipline of testing the predictions of the theory against the real world.

Peter Higgs' understanding of and insight into the world of subatomic particles led him to predict in 1964 the existence of the particle which bears his name, the Higgs boson. It was not until nearly 50 years later that the existence of the particle was confirmed at the CERN laboratory in Geneva. Gravity waves, recently detected from the collision of two black holes, have, more than a 100 years later, confirmed Einstein's prediction of their existence.

In macroeconomics the picture is categorically different and the difference is fatal to its claims to 'hard' scientific status. There are almost as many economic universes as there are macroeconomists. What's more many of them directly contradict each other. In his book, '**Economics: the User's Guide**', **Ha-Joon Chang** describes the great variety of alternative macroeconomic universes on offer. Here is his list of the major macroeconomic sects now vying for attention and influence:

- Classical,

- Neo-Classical,

- Marxist,

- Developmentalist,

- Austrian,

- Schumpeterian,

- Keynesian,

- Institutionalist,

- Behaviouralist.

Chang also provides a useful and illuminating cross-referencing table of the different viewpoints of each of these macroeconomic sects on major economic factors. Thus Individuals are 'selfish and rational' if you subscribe to the Classical doctrine but 'not very rational, driven by habits and animal spirits' for Keynesians. The World is 'complex and uncertain' if you are a macroeconomic Austrian or Keynesian but 'certain' if your macroeconomic worldview is Marxist. Again, economic policy recommendations are 'free market' if you are a classical or Austrian follower but interventionist if you are a Keynesian and socialist/centralized if you are Marxist.

These contradictions and permutations would have the makings of an amusing party game except for the very serious fact that the economic policies of governments, affecting the lives and well-being of a country's citizens in the most direct and important way, depend on the shifting dominance of one or other of these very different theoretical belief-systems. As forceful personalities rise to become economic advisers to governments, they confidently assert the superior validity of the macroeconomic theory they believe in and shape government economic policy to fit it. Thus their doctrinal creeds come to affect the lives of hundreds of millions.

Petri Dishes and Lab Rats

In his book '**Economics Rules**' **Dani Rodrik** states that 'It is difficult to see how economy-wide experiments could be performed that would test macroeconomic questions, for example on the role of fiscal or exchange rate policy'. This is the opposite of the truth. The history of economic policy in the developed and emerging economies shows that national economies have for long been treated by Economics advisers to governments as petri dishes or lab rats for a whole series of large-scale experiments. Contrary to Rodrik's belief that large-scale, economy-wide experiments are impossible, what we have in fact seen throughout history is widespread undisciplined testing in the real world of numerous macroeconomic theories, as many governments of differing political stripes have undertaken or imposed on their citizens a wide variety of macroeconomic policies.

In the early twentieth century these experiments were conducted by politicians. The former Soviet Union from its inception pursued a nation-wide experiment in Marxist/socialist Economics, with the elimination of private property and the centralization of economic control, to be run in the supposed interests of the nation. This and the forced adoption of collective farming methods led to multiple millions of deaths. The catastrophic experience of the Weimar republic in Germany was a textbook example of the consequences of believing that simply printing money was a viable solution to poverty - a cautionary tale now being enthusiastically replayed in Zimbabwe and in Venezuela. More recently the economic consequences of the Cultural Revolution in China were catastrophic, causing deaths in the tens of millions.[1]

Since the time of Keynes (reflecting the almost universal professional and intellectual respect accorded to his success in crafting a policy to prevent a repeat of the economic disaster of the Great Depression) theoretical macroeconomists have been granted more power to influence and dictate the management of national economies.[2]

In the 1960s, deficit-spending - Keynes' recommended solution to a collapse in private sector demand - was again expected to produce the desirable twin results of growth and high employment. This expectation lasted until inflation took off in the 1970s. Then inflation became the bogey-man and macroeconomic policy shifted to the control of inflation at all costs. For a long while this policy appeared to work well (with the great help of globalization and the IT revolution) but it was comprehensively derailed by the Crisis of 2008 and its long aftermath. After the Crisis macroeconomic policy concern shifted to the prevention of deflation and the threat of debt-deflation, as the developed economies have struggled under unprecedented mountains of debt.

Presently, central banks in the USA and other developed economies continue to be more concerned by the persistent lack of inflation than by its vigor, and higher inflation is now seen as a desirable target rather than a lethal danger. With growth still weak and interest rates still at very low levels, this leaves them in the difficult position of having no monetary ammunition (in the form of a reduction in interest rates and easier credit) in case another recession threatens. Global debt, both public and private, has climbed back to levels exceeding those before the Crisis, putting additional pressure on governments to keep rates low.[3]

As described in Chapter 7, macroeconomic policies pursued in the developed economies have historically seen the application of a series of theoretical 'orthodoxies', changing with the shifts in academic fashion. Typically, the reason behind these shifts has been the discrediting of the earlier theory by the realization or discovery that economic behavior is in fact significantly different from, or much more complex than, what the earlier theory predicted.

Thus, taking a wider and longer view of history, the populations of many countries have been the victims of economic policy experiments by governments and autocrats of one kind or another but also by macroeconomists. These experiments have had mainly catastrophic consequences. The disastrous experience of central planning in the Soviet Union and the Soviet bloc economies, the collapses of Zimbabwe and currently Venezuela are cases in point. It remains to be seen whether the present authoritarian economic rule in China survives the country's increasing loss of economic competitiveness and problematic demographic profile.

The Warm Bath of Irrelevance

If the vigorous existence (and even growth) of a multitude of contradictory economic universes demonstrates anything it is that the methods of Economics lack the intellectual rigor to sort sound economic wheat from pretentious chaff. As **Steve Keen** comments: 'the so-called science of Economics is a mélange of myths that make the Ptolemaic earth-centric view of the solar system look positively sophisticated by comparison'.

Chapter 8: Notes

1. In the UK, the enthusiasm for government intervention (and government ownership) after the Second World War led to the UK's treading the Hayekian road to serfdom and becoming the 'sick man of Europe' until Margaret Thatcher forthrightly pursued aggressive free market policies and restored growth. Famously, the Times of London published in 1981 a letter signed by 364 economists deploring the shift in policy and predicting economic disaster.
2. As noted in Chapter 1, Part 2, their influence grew strongly after the apparent success of the Great Moderation in the 1980s and '90s.
3. The depressed economic conditions still prevailing in much of the Eurozone seem a clear example of the willingness of political elites to sacrifice the populations in their care to the unreflective and inflexible application of ill-conceived economic policies.

Chapter 9

BLINDED BY NON-SCIENCE

'Most of what appears in the best journals of economics is unscientific rubbish.' **Deirdre McCloskey, The Secret Sins of Economics.**

'Given the travesties of logic and anti-empiricism that have been committed in its name, it would be an insult to the other sciences to give economics even a tentative membership of that field.' **Steve Keen, Debunking Economics.**

'Economics is essentially a moral science and not a natural science.' **J. M. Keynes, Letter to Roy Harrod, July 16th,** 1938.

'What economics really is, is a political argument. It is not – and can never be – a science.' **Ha-Joon Chang, Economics: the User's Guide.**

'If economics is to be practically relevant, there must be some concrete truths in which we can place confidence.' **Mark Blaug, Confessions of an Unrepentant Popperian.**

PART 1: IS ECONOMICS A REAL SCIENCE?

With the exception of a very few clear-thinking skeptics, economists have wished to regard the theories they develop as having the validity and standing of discoveries in the physical sciences. Some economists have delivered more illuminating theories than others but the vast majority share this desire for the validation and authority given by scientific status and many have come to believe it. (**Keynes**, who was profoundly skeptical of the scientific status of Economics, was an exception to this rule.) Furthermore economists have been very happy to encourage politicians and the general public to accept that their economic pronouncements merit the respect given to genuine science.

The disastrous failure of almost the entire Economics profession in not foreseeing, and recommending steps to prevent, the global Crisis of 2008 has focused a well-deserved light on the validity of Economics and on its status as a 'science'. Misled by the strong, steady expansion of the Golden Age of Growth during the 1980s and '90s, the world had accepted uncritically the claims of the Economics profession that they were responsible for it. Much more fancifully and dangerously, the world also accepted that economists had solved conclusively the essential economic problem of delivering durable, non-inflationary growth. The complacent hubris of the profession was summed up in the 2003 statement by Robert Lucas quoted at the head of Chapter 1, Part 2: 'The central problem of depression-prevention has been solved and has in fact been solved for many decades'.

The Crisis of 2008 comprehensively exploded this complacency and the fundamental question of the scientific status and validity of Economics has re-emerged as a matter for critical attention. If the vast majority of practicing economists had utterly failed to foresee the Crisis, what validity could they claim for the scientific status of Economics? So far from being true scientists, comparable to chemists or physicists in their methods and in the accumulation of a growing body of reliable, empirically-tested knowledge, the Crisis showed economists to be no better (in fact, according to **Philip Tetlock**, considerably worse) than the proverbial dart-throwing monkeys.

This has, rightly, put economists on the defensive and generated a lot of very welcome soul-searching. Earlier chapters have described the fundamental methodological shortcomings of the methods of Economics but besides these intrinsic flaws economists now need to justify not only the social usefulness of the profession but the fundamental validity of its scientific status.

Underlying the misplaced confidence in the validity of Economics has been the pretty well universal public acceptance of the economists' claim not just that Economics is a science but, more than this, that it deserves to rank with the physical 'hard' sciences. If this belief is accurate, it has seemed natural to accept that economists really are steadily increasing and improving our knowledge and understanding of how economies work and thereby steadily improving our ability to manage and control them for the greater benefit of mankind. The success of the Golden Age of Growth not only encouraged economists to bask in complacent self-esteem for their great wisdom and social value but misled both economists and the public at large into accepting unquestioningly the 'Economics is a true science' claim.

Reflective economists who have given some thought to the intellectual basis of their subject have been deeply skeptical of its scientific status. **Keynes**, the father of modern macroeconomics, always believed that Economics was a moral science and not one of the natural, 'hard' sciences. He believed that a good economist must be 'in some degree mathematician, historian, statesman and philosopher.' For him, Economics deals with 'motives, expectations and psychological uncertainties'. In the same vein, in his book, Economics: The User's Guide, the Cambridge academic economist **Ha-Joon Chang** regards Economics as, essentially, a political argument. Even **Paul Samuelson**, the author of the most popular standard university textbook for Economics students, who laid the foundations of mathematical economic theory, remarked in 1995 that 'Economics has never been a science'. He added the rider '…and it is even less so now than a few years ago', in reaction to the sorcerer's-apprentice flood of elaborate, abstract, vacuous, mathematizing which was even then taking over Economics.

The arguments why Economics is not a hard science have been comprehensively set out in books by some practicing economists. Interestingly, these books are few in number. The number of practicing economists who question the scientific basis of their subject and who have been ready to express this doubt in published books is, by comparison with the number of practicing economists, extremely small - almost as small, indeed, as the tiny roll-call of economists who foresaw the Crisis of 2008. It does not seem out of place to attribute this to the unwillingness of the large army of practicing economists to step off the great academic Economics gravy-train.

The most readable and comprehensive explanations of the flawed claims of Economics to be a hard science are given in two recent books: **Debunking Economics,** by **Steve Keen,** long but thorough[1] and **The Secret Sins of Economics,** by **Deirdre McCloskey**, short and very readable. Both Keen and McCloskey are fully fledged academic economists at the summit of their profession.

PART 2: STATISTICAL DATA: SIGNIFICANT AND MEANINGFUL OR MEANINGLESS AND INSIGNIFICANT?

'Regression analysis has turned out to be one of the most effective tools for divining economic cause and effect .... Regression equations as well as economic identities .... are the most prominent inputs of our macroeconomic models.' **Alan Greenspan, The Map and The Territory**.

'Statistical significance is not observing. Empirical economics is dominated by simple errors in statistical significance. Physics and Chemistry, though of course highly numerical, hardly ever use statistical significance. Economists .... use it compulsively.' **Deirdre McCloskey, The Secret Sins of Economics.**

'Regression analysis is more art than science.' **Steve Levitt** and **Stephen Dubner, Freakonomics**.

'There is one striking empirical fact about this whole literature, and that is that there is not one single empirical fact in it.' **Steve Keen, Debunking Economics.**

As Alan Greenspan admits in his book on the Crisis, The Map and the Territory, economists, unlike natural scientists, are unable to ground their forecasts in the sort of constant factual values which enable us to calculate with great precision the detailed physical structure and life-cycles of remote stars, the intricacies of chemical and biological reactions or the times of tides. As the economist **John Hicks** recognized: 'There are no such constants in economics ..... The economic world ..... is inherently in a state of flux.'[2]

In the absence of the kind of 'hard', empirically-validated evidence used in the physical sciences economists have had to find an alternative basis for their theories. The solution they have adopted is to use statistics. When economists seek to predict how economies, markets and individuals will react to new economic policy moves the method they have chosen is to use historical statistics of what happened in the past as a reliable guide to what will happen in the future.

As the quotation by Alan Greenspan at the head of this section confirms, this approach is one of the fundamental methods the US Federal Reserve relies on, as indeed it is for central banks and finance ministries across the globe, in forecasting the economic results of their policy moves. The future, they assume, can be relied on to be pretty much the same as the past. The great attraction of this method of course is that it provides sets of data values which macroeconomists can use as the basis for their models: it enables the use of mathematics to 'solve' their equations and thereby 'validate' their models.

There are three problems with this approach:

- the fallacy of equating statistical significance with empirical evidence,

- the inherent difficulty of accurately measuring any economic factor, and

- the fallacy of assuming that past patterns of behavior can safely be relied on to hold good into the future.

These problems are fundamental and serious yet they are pervasive in Economics.

i) The Statistical Significance Fallacy

Statisticians will admit, if pressed, that the behavioral patterns they identify do not have the validity of plain empirical evidence. Nonetheless, they claim, the patterns and correlations thrown up by the study of past data are 'statistically significant'. What they mean by this is that for Economics (and for other social sciences) the patterns of behavior apparent in the historical statistical data are as reliable as real empirical evidence and that they can therefore be validly used as a basis for forecasts and predictions.[3] Most of the claims made by statisticians and adopted by economists (that statistical significance is as valid as empirical evidence) spring from this basic fallacy.[4]

Use of this fallacious method has become pervasive in Economics. In a study of all the empirical articles in the *American Economic Review* in the 1980s it was discovered that fully 96% of them confused statistical significance and substantive significance.[5] The quotation by Alan Greenspan at the head of this chapter confirms that nothing has changed since this study and that this flawed, fundamentally unscientific prejudice still prevails in Economics.

ii) Measuring Economic Factors: How Long is a Piece of String?

The inherent difficulties of reliably measuring most economic behavior have been described earlier (see Chapter 6). Most economic factors are simply too complex and variable to be measured reliably enough to enable realistic calculation of cause and effect in Economics.

iii) Inertia: Tomorrow will be Pretty Much the Same as Yesterday

'Never underestimate the power of inertia.' **Richard Thaler, Nudge.**

The vast majority of professional economic forecasts are simple projections of the past into the future. Economists assume that the correlations and relationships which have been 'discovered' in the historical data by the flawed statistical process described above are a reliable basis for predicting identical future behavior. Besides the flaws in this process there is an additional consequence. If you systematically accept statistics on how economic agents reacted to past policy moves as a reliable predictor of how they will react to similar moves in future, you are in effect accepting that the primary and dominant motive of human economic behavior is inertia.[6] The quote above from **Richard Thaler**, though it referred to the much narrower field of Behavioral Economics, seems perfectly appropriate as a comment on the methods of macroeconomists.

PART 3: UNCERTAINTY AND RISK: STATISTICAL
SIGNIFICANCE AND THE FINANCIAL MARKETS

The most prolific use of the concept of statistical significance has been made by participants in the world's financial markets. In fact, it is fair to say that the failure (or perhaps unwillingness) to distinguish between statistical significance and risk, taken together with uncontrolled credit, was largely responsible for the Crisis of 2008.

The symbol used by financial market participants to specify measurements of the risk of a financial asset is the Greek letter sigma Σ. The sigma value of a financial asset is a measure of its price volatility - the propensity of the price of the asset to change. If the price of an asset swings about a lot it is considered more risky than an investment with less, more stable price variation. There are gradations of volatility, measured as increasing deviations from a stable mean. Higher sigma values indicate greater volatility - a greater probability of change and therefore, by this calculation, both greater risk and also greater improbability of occurrence.

As computer power exploded in the 1980s the financial and investment industry enthusiastically adopted statistical risk calculations to lend what seemed to be 'scientific' support to numerous investment strategies. Banks calculated their Value-at-Risk figure (VAR) as an apparently reliable measure of the riskiness of the institutions and of their vulnerability to events. As the Great Moderation led to an explosion in the extent and number of derivative contracts in financial markets of all kinds (equities, bonds, commodities, credit, foreign exchange etc.) investment managers and hedge funds used VAR calculations to justify exposures to these instruments for both themselves and their clients. Buttressing the enormous volume of these contracts was the assumption that VAR calculations were reliable enough to justify the use of greater and greater leverage without a commensurate increase in risk.[7]

Black Swans: once in 100 million years and three times in a week

When the music stopped abruptly in September, 2008, the party stopped for a large number of foolish virgins like Lehman Brothers. At the time of its bankruptcy Lehman Brothers' capital was leveraged nearly 30 times and they were far from being alone. As noted, earlier, in 1998, the much-vaunted hedge fund Long Term Capital Management had based the 40-to-1 expansion of its balance sheet before its collapse on the supposedly valid risk calculations thrown up by the mathematics of statistical significance and improbability. Yet there was nothing new or unfamiliar in the reasons for the collapse. In 2002, six years before the Crisis, **Warren Buffett** had described financial derivatives as weapons of mass destruction.

In the months before the Crisis, events were occurring in the financial market place which, by statistical reckoning, were so improbable that they should have occurred only once in many million years. David Viniar, Chief Financial Officer of Goldman Sachs, lamented in August, 2007: 'We were seeing things that were 25-standard deviation moves, several days in a row.' A sigma of 25 is absurdly improbable - even a sigma of 7, if it is accurate, means the probability of one single occurrence in more than 3 billion years.[8] The mistake the financial masters of the universe were making was failing to distinguish between risk, which can, more or less, be measured and uncertainty, which cannot. The confused thinking which led to this disastrous and widespread failure has been decisively skewered by **Nassim Nicholas Taleb** in his book, **The Black Swan**.[9]

PART 4 : EMPIRICISM: MICROECONOMICS
AND BEHAVIORAL ECONOMICS

'To understand human economic behavior we clearly need to get back to studying Humans rather than Econs.' Paraphrase of **Richard Thaler, Misbehaving**.

'The whole intention of empirical economics is to force theory down to Earth.' **George Akerlof.**

A more fruitful approach to validating Economics as a science has come from the field of micro/behavioral economics. The underlying thesis of this approach is that the analysis and explanation of the processes underlying human behavior in small-scale, limited, even intimately personal, real-life, economic-choice situations can enable meaningful and successful predictions of their behavior. The wishful further claim is that these insights, with their empirical basis, can validate the scientific status of the theoretical abstractions which are the product of Economics on the large scale - macroeconomics.

In 1970 the economist **George Akerlof** published a short paper entitled **'The Market for Lemons'**. His paper analyzed the effects in the used automobile market of the very different information available to the seller and to the buyer of a used car as to the car's real condition. This was the first paper to focus on what is called 'informational asymmetry' and its effects in markets and in social policy. At the time, Akerlof's paper had great difficulty in finding a publisher. Both the *American Economic Review* and the *Review of Economic Studies* rejected the paper for 'triviality' while the *Journal of Political Economy* reviewers rejected it as 'incorrect'. It is now one of the most-cited papers in economic theory and the most downloaded economic journal paper of all time.[10] The importance of 'informational asymmetry' in economic behavior was recognized by the award of the Nobel Economics Prize in 2001 to Akerlof, jointly with Joseph Stiglitz and Michael Spence. Akerlof's paper has had a profound influence on several fields of Economics and, as the Nobel award indicated, the validity and importance of analyzing human economic behavior at the small-scale, basic level has received growing recognition.

Following **Akerlof**'s paper the attention of economists to the analysis of real human behavior on a limited, day-to-day level has grown enormously. The appearance in 2005 of **'Freakonomics'** by the economist **Steve Levitt** and **Stephen Dubner** gave an additional boost to the wider professional and public awareness and acceptance of small-scale, empirically-based analysis. **'Freakonomics'** describes in persuasive and very readable terms numerous exercises, backed by solid empirical tests, demonstrating the real economic structures and relationships underlying a number of social conditions (e.g. the link between the decision in Roe v. Wade and the subsequent drop in crime). The book was an enormous and well-deserved popular success and the authors followed up with two further books in the same vein: **'Superfreakonomics'** in 2009 and **'Think Like a Freak'**, in 2014.

Another economist, **Richard Thaler**, had for some time been working in the same behavioral arena.[11] In two books, **'Nudge'** and **'Misbehaving'**, published in 2008 and 2015 respectively, he set out at greater length the findings of his analytical work and the potential benefits of the behavioral approach in the social policy field. The insights recorded by **Thaler** in his books are all the more compelling for being based on empirically-verified behavior. It is difficult not to agree with **Thaler's** call for more of the evidence-based Economics which is the stock-in-trade of **Behavioral Economics**.

Behavioral Economics (or what the economist **Gary Becker** has described as the application of an 'economic' approach) has tapped a productive and illuminating vein of human economic behavior and identified a number of reliably consistent psychological responses to many economic-choice situations. In many cases the responses are consistent and persuasive enough to have encouraged some governments to adopt policies relying on what **Thaler** calls the '**Nudge**' factor to promote socially beneficial behavior.[12,13] Further confirmation of the real social utility of this microeconomic approach was given by the award of the 2019 Nobel Economics Prize to the team of **Michael Kremer, Abhijit Banerjee and Esther Duflo** for their successful use of systematically tested empirical data to improve policies in the areas of health and education. Thus, Behavioral Economics and economic policy have moved towards each other.

The work of **Angus Deaton**, awarded the Nobel Economics Prize in 2015, has focused very usefully on the links between patterns of personal consumption, poverty and welfare. Also, as **Richard Thaler** confirms in the concluding chapter of his book '**Misbehaving**', a new generation of economists has adopted the practice of moving from behavioral evidence first to theory development second. Additional evidence of the shift in focus from macroeconomic theorizing towards empirically-validated analysis is afforded by the work and career of **Jean Tirole**, awarded the Nobel Economics Prize in 2014. In his book '**Economics for the Common Good**', published in English in 2017, he devotes 1½ pages (out of more than 500) to macroeconomics.

From Micro to Macro?

Yet the examples and behavioral responses presented by **Thaler** and the **Kremer, Banerjee and Duflo** team are all of day-to-day choices on a very small scale.[14] Unfortunately for the idea that microeconomics can deliver a solid empirical basis for macroeconomics, the small-scale patterns of personal behavior in limited situations which are the foundation of microeconomics cannot serve as a solid and reliable basis for large-scale economic responses at the whole-economy level of macro-economic policy.

Economists Disagree

Needless to say, the assessments of the questionable validity of Economics as a 'hard science' have met strong opposition from the vast majority of practicing economists who, with good reason, see these criticisms as dangerously undermining their status as acknowledged experts. If the idol can be shown to have feet of such weak clay, the entire authority of the 'profession' goes by the board. Thus the overwhelming impression to be gained from the published Economics literature, including the leading academic journals and the most popular university Economics textbooks, is that the last thing the vast majority of practicing economists are prepared to do is to acknowledge the errors and limits of their subject and its usefulness. To do so of course would kill the golden goose of pretentious imposture which has allowed them such agreeable, well-paid careers.

Regrettably, this complacency as to the valid scientific status of Economics has been greatly reinforced by the global public-relations impact of the annual award of the **Nobel Prize for Economic Sciences** (see Chapter 10). The annual PR ballyhoo-fest attending this event has served from its inception, and still serves, to inflate undeservedly the respect and attention paid to the recipients of the Prize in the minds of the lay public (and, alas, in the minds of the politicians they advise).

Conclusion

Microeconomics may justifiably persuade us that economists are of some social use after all but in the really important field of macroeconomics, where reliable and lasting success would durably improve economic management and thereby the living standards of large numbers of human beings, the Economics profession has failed abysmally. If economists are to deserve respect they must deliver successful policies and deliver them not just once by happy chance but reliably over time in different economic conditions.

If the same conditions can, and regularly do, generate widely different responses to macroeconomic policy measures, and if most economists' forecasts are seriously inaccurate, Economics cannot be a 'hard' science. But if it is not a hard science what is it? The most accurate and appropriate scientific term to describe macroeconomic theories and explanations would seem to be that they are, at best, conjectures.[15]

Chapter 9: Notes

1. See in particular Chapter 8: There is Madness in their Method.
2. John Hicks, Causality in Economics, 1979. Hicks had made the same point in his Nobel Prize acceptance speech in 1972: 'Our science colleagues find permanent truths; economists, who deal with the daily actions of men and the consequences of these, can rarely hope to find the same permanency.'
3. The typical argument goes: in 99% (or 95%, or 97%) of the occurrences of this policy change in the past, the result was X. Consequently there is a statistically significant probability of the same outcome in future. Accordingly, we are justified in predicting that X will occur in future if the same policy is applied now.
4. As Deirdre McCloskey comments: 'Statistical significance is hardly ever used in physics and chemistry. Economists and sociologists use it compulsively, mechanically and erroneously.'
5. Reported by D. McCloskey, The Secret Sins of Economics.
6. In fact, as noted earlier, there is considerable evidence from within the Economics profession that economies typically respond to a policy move differently the second time around from how they reacted the first time. Goodhart's Law, named after its proposer/discoverer Charles Goodhart, then Chief Economist at the Bank of England, is expressed as follows: 'when a measure becomes a target, it ceases to be a good measure'. The reason, of course, is that economic agents adapt and vary their behavior to take account of it.
7. Another example of the perverted use of statistics by the financial sector to lend a specious scientific gloss to justify profitable business (which later collapsed) is the so-called Gaussian copula. The use of the word 'Gaussian' refers to the symmetric distribution bell-curve described by the German mathematician Carl Gauss. In 2000 David Li, a JP Morgan Chase statistician, devised a method for

measuring, supposedly reliably, the correlation between, and therefore the aggregate risk of, very different mortgage securities. If you want to dig deeper in this subject See: 'Recipe for Disaster: the Formula that Killed Wall Street' by Felix Salmon, Wired Magazine, February 23rd, 2009, and if you want to dig really deep in this subject, see; 'The Formula that Killed Wall Street', by D. Mackenzie and T Spears, Edinburgh University, June, 2012.

8. See: https://arxiv.org/ftp/arxiv/papers/1103/1103.5672.pdf.
9. Nassim Nicholas Taleb, The Black Swan, 2010.
10. For example: organ donation, various environmental issues, tax compliance.
11. Interestingly, Thaler sees Keynes as the true father of Behavioral Economics, citing Keynes' famous 'beauty contest' theory as confirmation of his belief in the importance of the behavior of market agents.
12. Also, although there are consistent patterns in human behavior in response to these economic situations, there is still considerable variability in the responses of different agents to a given economic situation and also, even if less so, of the same agent on different occasions.
13. Perhaps because their theories flew in the face of the prevailing macroeconomic orthodoxy, only two awards of the Nobel Economics Prize have been to behavioral economists: Herbert Simon (1978) and Daniel Kahnemann and Vernon Smith (2002).
14. See 'What is Next?' in Thaler's 'Misbehaving'.
15. Even this term is somewhat flattering to the status of Economics. Many famous conjectures in mathematics and hard science have been decisively confirmed (or disproved) by later experiment or analysis.

Chapter 10

———✥———

THE PRETENCE OF WISDOM:
THE NOBEL ECONOMICS PRIZE

'…. the Nobel Prize confers on an individual an authority which in Economics no man ought to possess. This does not matter in the natural sciences. Here the influence exercised by an individual is chiefly an influence on his fellow experts; and they will soon cut him down to size if he exceeds his competence. But the influence of the economist that mainly matters is an influence over laymen: politicians, journalists, civil servants and the public generally. There is no reason why a man who has made a distinctive contribution to economic science should be omnicompetent on all problems of society - as the press tends to treat him, till in the end he may himself be persuaded to believe.' **Friedrich von Hayek, Nobel Banquet Speech**, 1974.

'While economic models, it has been shown, work hardly better than random guesses or the intuition of cab drivers, physics can predict a wide range of phenomena with a tenth decimal precision. Every time I have questioned [economic] methods I have been abruptly countered with: 'they have the Nobel.' **Nassim Nicholas Taleb, The Pseudoscience Hurting Markets**, 2007.

'In the quest for valid knowledge … it is well to ignore black boxes, the magic of prizes and the lure of immutable laws.' **Avner Offer and Gabriel Soderberg, The Nobel Factor**, 2015.

'Many of the economists who have received the Alfred Nobel Memorial Prize for Economic Science work within the paradigms of rational choice theory and statistical modelling. Yet it is a noteworthy fact that not a single one of them has been awarded the prize for confirmed empirical predictions.' **Jon Elster**, **Excessive Ambitions**, 2009.

The Nobel Prize Syndrome

In 1974 the Nobel Economics Prize was awarded, jointly with **Gunnar Myrdal**, to **Friedrich von Hayek**, the free-market Austrian economist. The prize, for 'Outstanding Contributions to Economic Science', had been established and endowed in 1968 by the Sveriges Riksbank, the Swedish central bank, on the occasion of the bank's 300th anniversary, as an addition to the existing awards for contributions to branches of science like Chemistry, Physics and Medicine and, in the humanities, for Literature and Peace. The award was given to both honorees for 'their pioneering work in the theory of money and economic fluctuations and for their penetrating analysis of the interdependence of economic, social and institutional phenomena'.

The award of the prize to Hayek was controversial and much criticized, particularly within the Economics profession. Gunnar Myrdal, Hayek's co-honoree, a Swede and an old-school social democrat and advocate of public spending who later served in the Swedish government, was later especially critical, wanting the prize abolished because it had been given to 'such reactionaries as Hayek and Milton Friedman'. However, if there is an argument for questioning the legitimacy of the Economics prize it should rest not on political disagreement but, much more validly, on the meagerness and questionable human significance of the prize-winners' contributions.

*Well: How Many Angels **Can** you Get on the Head of a Pin?*

Since its inception the rollcall of winners of the Economics prize has included more than 70 economists. On the face of it their expertise has covered a wide range of subjects. Yet reading the citations for most of the Economics prizewinners is to enter a shadow realm of abstract, theoretical pedantry entirely out of touch with the real world or with the welfare of real human beings. Analysis of the Prize citations shows that, with very few exceptions, the work for which the prize has been awarded has not been improvements in economic policy which have led to an improvement in human welfare but minimal refinements of the analytical methods of abstract economic theory. The overriding impression is one of intense, abstract navel-gazing and finicky nit-picking having no relation to the real world.

Thus the first prize, awarded in 1969 to **Ragnar Frisch** and **Jan Tinbergen**, was for 'the development and application of dynamic models for the analysis of economic processes'. A year later **Paul Samuelson** was awarded the prize for 'the scientific work through which he has developed static and dynamic economic theory and actively contributed to raising the level of analysis in economic thought'. In 1987 **Robert Solow** won for 'his contributions to the theory of economic growth'. Other citations have included: 'For extending the domain of microanalysis' (**Gary Becker**, 1992), 'Theory and methods for analyzing selective samples' (**Heckman**, 2000), 'Analyses of markets with asymmetric information' (**Spence, Stiglitz, Akerlof**, 2001), 'Analyzing economic time series with time-varying volatility' (**Engle**, 2003). In 2013 the award went jointly to **Robert Shiller** and to the team of **Eugene Fama** and **Lars Hensen** for 'Their Empirical Analysis of Asset Prices' (ignoring entirely the fact that their conclusions were essentially contradictory).[1]

As noted, very occasionally the Nobel Committee has awarded the Economics prize for contributions from social science specialists with a tangential connection to Economics. Thus in 2002 **Daniel Kahnemann** won the prize for work illuminating the psychology of human judgment and decision-making. More recently **Angus Deaton** was awarded the prize in 2015 for work on consumption, poverty and welfare and in 2017 **Richard Thaler** won the prize for his work on Behavioral Economics.[2,3] Mainly, though, the award of the Prize has been for elaborate and abstract refinements of the analytical methods used by academic economists working within the bounds of accepted economic orthodoxy.

What the Economics prize has never been awarded for is any significant improvement in actual economic management or even a single instance of a substantial, verifiable improvement in human welfare, something like 'for enabling developed economies to grow by an extra 1% per annum for ten years', for example, or 'for lifting 250 million subsistence peasants out of poverty'. As the quote from John Elster at the head of this chapter points out, not a single award has been for confirmed empirical predictions. Yet the purpose of the Nobel Prizes, as set out by Alfred Nobel when he launched them in 1902, was to give public acknowledgement (and a considerable sum of money) to advances in Science which had notably improved the human condition.[4]

Real Science and Pseudo-Science

The Nobel Prize in Economic Sciences bears a considerable measure of responsibility for the view that Economics is a real science. The creation and history of the Economics prize has greatly encouraged the mistaken view that Economics can justifiably be considered a science on an authoritative par with the natural sciences like Physics, Chemistry or Medicine for which Alfred Nobel originally created his prize. These days whenever a Nobel Economics prizewinner is mentioned in the press delivering his opinion on some issue, the tag 'Nobel Economics Laureate' is now invariably added, with the strong implication that it conveys a valid stamp of scientific authority.

As noted earlier, economists desperately wish to be accepted as real scientists (see Chapter 9). The comparison of the cited reasons for the awards of the Economics prize with the awards for the physical sciences is revealing. It is rather as though **Peter Higgs** was awarded the Physics prize not for accurately predicting, more than 50 years earlier, the now-proven existence of the Higgs boson but for suggesting a more elaborate technique for designing a minor and insignificant part of a machine which might or might not turn out to be useful in practice. There is therefore an enormous gap between the typical contributions made by most of the Nobel Economics prize winners, which have focused on minutiae of theoretical economic explanation, and the major problems of economic management, so-called macroeconomics, which deal with growth, employment and inflation - the central concerns of human welfare.

Comparing the development of the theory and practice of Economics since the Second World War with the advances in many fields of the physical sciences makes very clear the enormous chasm between the real and dramatic advances achieved in many fields of applied science and the inflated claims of economists.

Consider manned flight, for example, one of the myriad branches of science and engineering which have recorded enormous progress over the last century. One has only to consider the extraordinary advance from the Wright Brothers through the Spitfire and Messerschmitt of World War II to the Boeing Dreamliner, not to mention the Voyager spacecraft, the Apollo moonshots and the Hubble telescope, to see how abysmally the Economics profession has failed to achieve even a modest improvement in macroeconomic management. In fact, as the Crisis of 2008 and its aftermath demonstrate, so far from delivering better living conditions for mankind, Economics has failed even to fulfil the first precept of the Hippocratic Oath and do no harm. It would be nice if macroeconomists could point to even a few small improvements in the management of developed economies or even agree on how to avoid serious past errors in economic management. Yet here we are, 12 years after the financial crisis of 2008 with growth in the developed economies still significantly weaker than its pre-crisis level in Europe, Japan and the USA.

Contradictions

There are many contemporary examples of the uncertainty, unreliability and contradictions which are still the defining hallmarks of macroeconomics. Two major examples are, first, the comparison between the policy followed by the USA after the Great Depression of 1929/30 and the policy adopted by the Federal Reserve and the Treasury after the Crisis of 2008 and, secondly, the comparison between the harsh monetary policy adopted by the IMF in the 1980s and '90s to resolve the frequent crises in the developing economies since World War II and the IMF's current disapproval of the continued policy of severe austerity being imposed by the ECB and the European Commission to solve the persistent economic imbalances in the Eurozone.

Ben Bernanke's doctoral thesis subject and his major area of academic focus was the Great Depression and there was a widespread expectation, with his appointment, that this academic specialization gave him significant expertise in devising effective measures to counteract the effects of the Great Recession. The great mistake of the measures adopted to solve the earlier Great Depression is judged now to be the severe monetary squeeze applied by Hoover and Mellon. The opposite policy has been followed in the USA ever since the 2008 crisis, with liquidity being pumped into the economy in massive quantities. It is undeniable that without QE the financial crisis would have turned into a catastrophic global collapse. The interconnection of financial markets (foreign exchange, interbank lending, financial asset investment), the massive growth in world trade (trade finance/letters of credit) and the similar strong growth in foreign direct investment flows, had all generated an expansion and deepening of interconnectivity which would have spread the crisis across the globe.

Yet it is clear that the massive monetary stimulus applied since the Crisis did not generate a durable return to prior levels of growth. Unemployment has remained a concern (if realistic measures are used), until very recently real wages had not risen since the Crisis, investment has fallen (in spite of rock-bottom interest rates and massive cash balances in corporate balance sheets) and growth has been at best mediocre. The geopolitical situation has not been greatly unfavorable - even allowing for a continuing slowdown in China - there are no major wars, protectionism is under control, so why has there been no return to growth? Posing the question is not so much to criticize the policy of QE as a failure, though there are quite a few economists who believe this, but to illustrate the inherent uncertainty of the process of cause and effect in macroeconomics.

The second example provides another clear illustration of this inherent uncertainty and of the major differences of policy which can spring from it. From time to time in the 1990s developing economies got into economic difficulties (the Far East crisis of late '90s, the Russian default of 1997, etc.). The most common economic feature of many of these events was a balance-of-payments crisis arising from growing external hard currency indebtedness and a resulting inability to service or repay these debts. Countries in difficulties turned to the IMF for assistance. At the time IMF policy for remedying these problems was harshly monetarist. Temporary funding was made available to countries in difficulties subject to the simultaneous imposition of a severe clampdown on consumer demand. Unrelenting austerity was held to be the solution to the problem. This was for a long while the orthodox policy response of the IMF to balance-of-payments crises.

Fast forward to today. Since the introduction of the Euro in 1999 the operation of the single currency has led to the growth of enormous commercial and financial imbalances between the members of the Eurozone and to the creation of corresponding, equally enormous, inter-member debts. There is no sign of these imbalances (which spring essentially from deep-rooted and long-standing social and cultural differences between the Eurozone member states) being smoothly or calmly resolved. The Eurozone authorities, and in particular the ECB, have from the start adopted a policy very similar to the harsh economic clampdown and controls imposed by the IMF on the unfortunate developing economies which got into difficulties in the last two decades of the last century.

It is ever more apparent that, since weaker Eurozone members cannot devalue, the consequence of the purblind EZ policy of imposing austerity as the solution to their excessive debts and imbalances is steadily growing human misery on a colossal scale. Complacent bureaucrats in Brussels together with national politicians, well insulated from the effects of their decisions by an almost total lack of political accountability (as well as generous remuneration packages), continue to insist on austerity as the path to economic health, a return to growth and the elimination of these countries' intra-zonal debts. The response to the prospect of the inevitable failure of these policies (which is likely before long to impact France) has been the time-honored response of the EZ authorities to difficult problems, a resort to pedicanitis, a.k.a. kicking-the-can-down-the-road, 'extend and pretend' - a steadfast refusal to address the problem and a feckless hope that 'something will turn up'.

Meanwhile the IMF has, finally, seen the light. Their former unbending commitment to the orthodoxy of austerity as the sovereign solution to the problems caused by economic mismanagement and excess external debt has given way, at least as regards their advice to the EZ, to a welcome if belated recognition of the dangerous irrelevance of austerity as a solution to the deep problems of the Eurozone.

The purpose of mentioning this fundamental change of strategy and change of view is that it is an excellent illustration of the dangers of regarding any macroeconomic policy proposals as the reliable product of a science, that is to say as proposals which are grounded in the solid, proven foundations of experience and which are reliably and durably valid for the purposes of official economic policy.

After receiving the Economics prize in Stockholm, **Hayek** delivered the customary acceptance speech. The year was 1974, soon after the start of the disastrous decade of the 1970s which saw the rate of inflation rocket, the collapse of global stock markets and widespread economic recession. Hayek's speech focused on the failure of economists to guide policy successfully. For him, economists 'have little cause for pride; as a profession we have made a mess of things'. The reason Hayek identified for this failure of Economics to be effective is that economic behavior is essentially too complex to permit reliable or comprehensive measurement but that economists continue to behave as though it isn't. The result, Hayek said, is 'scientism', pseudo-science, a belief that the methods of Economics are as valid as those of the physical sciences and that the results of economic theory can provide valid solutions to the problems of managing an economy.[5] The great tragedy is that the rest of mankind, and in particular government officials, still continue to accept the flawed, self-serving pronouncements of economists as a reliable and valid guide to official policy.

Hayek entitled his speech '**The Pretence of Knowledge**'. In the light of the disastrous track-record of economists, a more accurate title would be 'The Pretence of Wisdom'. Yet despite their calamitous failure economists continue to claim not only that Economics is a science but that familiarity with the fallacious methods of Economics is a prerequisite to prescribing valid economic policy proposals. It is fair to say that the main characteristics of the work of most Nobel Economics prizewinners are questionable method and irrelevance to the real concerns of mankind. Yet once they have won the prize, Nobel Economics laureates are uncritically accepted by the world's financial media (and in turn by the public) as fully qualified to pronounce authoritatively not only on matters of macroeconomic policy but on a wide range of social and political problems.[6]

Shamans and Witchdoctors

As their disastrous track-record continues to demonstrate, when it comes to recommending reliably successful policies macroeconomists are no more than witch-doctors - shamans casting their jumble of horse-feathers and chicken bones to the accompaniment of obscure mumbo-jumbo incantations, hoping to blind the credulous crowd with their opaque, pseudo-scientific pronouncements.[7]

Chapter 10: Notes

1. 'The Nobel Factor' by Avner Offer and Gabriel Soderberg, 2016, gives a comprehensive description of the history of the Nobel Prize for Economics with critical reflections on the questionable scientific and intellectual merits of the contributions of Prize winners.
2. George Akerlof's 1970 paper 'The Market for Lemons', on informational asymmetry, seems to be a forerunner of the development of Behavioral Economics as an acknowledged subset of Economics. The cited work of his co-laureates Joseph Stiglitz and Michael Spence also fall into this category.
3. These recent awards suggest that academic Economics may, finally, be moving away from vacuous abstraction and engaging with the real world; see Chapter 12. See also Note 7 below: the 2019 Economics Prize award for the first time rewarded real, socially-useful empirical achievement.
4. J. M. Keynes, had he lived, would have been a prime candidate for the Prize on this basis.
5. Hayek records the many fallacies which beset Economics, then and now: e.g. unquantifiability and the recourse to measurable but irrelevant factors; reductive

simplification to eliminate the essential complexity of economic behavior; the overuse of mathematics; pattern prediction as a substitute for empirical evidence, etc.

6. For example: Paul Krugman has a regular pulpit in the New York Times and comments on a wide variety of social and political matters; Lawrence Summers, one of the main agents of the 2008 Crisis, writes regular Op Ed pieces in the Financial Times. Another economist (and Nobel Economics prizewinner) who regularly comments publicly on a wide variety of political as well as economic issues is Joseph Stiglitz. (It was curious to see Stiglitz' election to a fellowship at All Souls College at Oxford. All Souls has for very long been, and is still, the gold standard of intellectual excellence in the UK and indeed globally. Stiglitz has had the sort of glittering career in many exalted positions in public life which the rise of Economics and economists over the last half century has propelled. His election seems to ignore not only the fundamentally questionable status of Economics as a genuine academic discipline but also the relatively trivial contribution of Stiglitz' work to the real welfare of mankind. In this of course he is far from being the only guilty party among Nobel Economics Prize laureates and practicing macroeconomists.)

7. Finally, the Economics Prize, in the 2019 award, gave recognition for the first time to academic work in Economics which has had verifiable socially beneficial results. The award to Abhijit Banerjee, Esther Duflo and Michael Kremer was for 'their experimental approach to alleviating global poverty'. Their research, which made systematic use of randomized controlled trials, led to empirically-backed policy recommendations which have been successfully adopted in the fields of education and health care.

Chapter 11

DENTISTS, ENGINEERS, PLUMBERS AND NOVELISTS

'An economist should be mathematician, historian, statesman and philosopher in some degree.' **John Maynard Keynes.**

There have been several attempts by prominent economists to restore the now uncertain status and authority of Economics and to re-establish the reputation of the subject as a socially useful 'science'. These attempts claim, on various grounds, that Economics is indeed a true science. The argument is that, even if its methods and processes are not as rigorous as those of the hard sciences, the claim of scientific status for Economics is nonetheless justified because economists are accumulating a growing body of tried-and-true advances in verifiable knowledge having useful application.

Analogies for Economics

Most arguments for Economics to be respected as a true science have taken the approach of argument by analogy – looking at the question of the validity and usefulness of Economics by comparing Economics and its methods to other service professions. What other profession or occupation can Economics fairly be compared to? **Keynes**, speaking in the early days of economic theory, hoped that as Economics developed, economists should seek to achieve the status and usefulness of a very simple, hum-drum occupation. Though he himself was supremely aware of the inherent uncertainty and variability of human economic behavior, he believed and expected that, once it had matured, Economics might reasonably aspire to the basic, useful status of a modest occupation like dentistry.

Along the same lines **Tim Harford**, in one of his weekly 'Undercover Economist' articles in the Financial Times recently debated this question and its history[1]. His article was a reaction to the frank public admission by Andy Haldane, Chief Economist at the Bank of England, that the failure of economists to foresee the 2008 Crisis was equivalent to the disastrous record of UK weather forecasters in failing to foresee the devastating UK hurricane of 1987.

Harford mentions two recent proposed analogies for Economics: first, that of Al Roth (a Nobel laureate in Economics) echoing the view of Robert Shiller, also a Nobel Economics laureate (see below), that economists should be seen as engineers and, secondly, the proposal of Esther Duflo that economists should be thought of as plumbers 'since plumbing is more practical than engineering'. She sees economists as not only installing the system but 'tinkering with it' after installation to deal with leaks and blockages.[2]

Economics as Engineering

Another argument by analogy for the scientific status of Economics has been made by Robert Shiller, former President of the American Economics Association. Shiller has proposed that an appropriate analogy for the methods and usefulness of Economics is the field of engineering. He argues that, like engineering, Economics proceeds and advances by a series of incremental discoveries, each of them adding improvements to the accuracy, relevance and social usefulness of Economics in the same way that scientific discoveries and advances have built on an established body of incremental performance improvements and discoveries in the engineering field.

This is fanciful in the extreme. As noted earlier, a simple comparison of the lamentable progress made by Economics (from its emergence as a separate subject more than 200 years ago, through its coming of age with the contributions of Keynes and its growth after World War II, the stumbles of the inflationary 1970s and the deceptive Golden Age of Growth in the 1980s and '90s, to the global Crisis of 2008 and its low-growth aftermath) with the development of flight, from the Wright Brothers to Concord, Boeing 747s, the Moon landing and the Voyager spacecraft now exiting the solar system, makes starkly clear how paltry, and even injurious, the achievements of Economics have been.

Alternatively, to take biology, the advance in hard knowledge from the discovery and development of penicillin and other life-saving drugs to the discovery of DNA by Watson, Crick and Franklin and the life-enhancing possibilities promised by stem-cell rejuvenation and now gene editing, makes clear the immense gulf between the achievements of real science in many varied fields and the meandering, contradictory and crisis-strewn course of Economics.

With the best will in the world it is extremely difficult to see these interpretations of Economics as the exercise of reliable, professional expertise. Nearly a century after **Keynes**, the simple effectiveness (and usefulness) of dentistry or similar low-level engineering occupations like vehicle repair or plumbing are decisively beyond the reach of Economics. The pretty well universal failure of the Economics profession to foresee the 2008 Crisis and the failure of the massive injections of liquidity by the world's central banks to return the major economies to normal growth, in accordance with the dominant economic model they swear by, have exploded the earlier respect for Economics. This accusation of failure and uselessness is, of course, vigorously resisted by the swelling numbers of economists in the world's finance ministries and central banks and in Academia.

All these analogies seek to demonstrate that, in spite of its repeated, disastrous failures, the 'profession' of Economics deserves to be considered a science and furthermore that it is of significant social use. Alas, none of the proposed analogies - dentistry, plumbing, engineering, auto-mechanics etc. – rings true: none of them successfully demonstrates either a valid 'hard' scientific status for Economics or the reliable social usefulness of the profession.

He said, he said, he said

As we have seen, the abundance of macroeconomic models and theories filling the pages of the Economics journals are often contradictory. Just to read the list of the multiple active schools of economic theory (see Chapter 8, **Ha-Joon Chang**) is to become aware of the contradictory and bewildering number and variety of explanatory models on offer, each with its claim to relevance and validity. Reading even summary explanations of the differences between them is confusing in the extreme. As noted, Chang provides a schematic diagram comparing the major characteristics of each of the schools in terms of their attitudes to major economic and social concepts (selfishness, rationality, production, consumption, individuals, classes, policy preferences etc.). It is rather as though the theories of the Babylonians, Thales of Miletus, the Druids, Copernicus, Galileo, Newton and the Flat-Earth society were all still in vigorous life and claiming equal scientific validity.

As noted in Chapter 7, **Dani Rodrik** believes that the many current macroeconomic models and theories are all useful since they offer explanations of, and solutions for, a wide variety of economic situations and problems. Taken together, he maintains, these models and theories make up a growing body of useful advances in economic management. Yet, as he admits, the usefulness of an economic model depends on judgment; the model does not stand by itself and cannot be relied on without human intervention.

None of these attempts to claim hard or quasi-hard scientific status for Economics is convincing. Shiller's engineering analogy is clearly mistaken, as a simple comparison with several branches of scientific achievement demonstrates. Rodrik's argument from usefulness may have some validity but, as an argument for the scientific status of Economics, is fatally undermined by his admission that human judgment is always necessary for applying any given economic model.

However, the conceptual problem facing economists is not only the difficulty of blending successfully the three principles referred to by Keynes: economic efficiency, social justice and individual liberty. For a start they are values which cannot be measured by reference to one single yardstick; in the lingo, they are not commensurable.

None of these quasi-scientific theories confronts squarely and overcomes the central problem which faces all Economics and which is particularly lethal for macroeconomists. It is the problem which goes to the heart of the 'Economics is a science' argument. Human reactions to economic situations not only differ, and differ significantly, as between individuals, let alone groups of individuals; they are subject to continuous change. They are, unavoidably, too variable to provide a solid basis for any durable, universally successful economic theory.[3]

Economics as Novel-Writing

If we are looking for analogies for Economics a much better example seems to be novel-writing. Like novelists, economists produce a succession of ever-changing descriptions and interpretations of human economic behavior. Like novelists, economists face a world which is continuously changing and human behavior which also shifts and adapts continuously.

If novel-writing is indeed a better analogy for what economists do, we can exercise our imaginations in categorizing the practitioners of the dismal 'science' into appropriate novelistic genres. We can compare the major figures of Economics, the individuals who are accepted as the founding fathers of the subject and who defined the principles of economic thinking, to the historical figures of literature whose achievement and humanity have withstood the critical test of time.

We can consider whether any of the major figures in the history of Economics correspond in their insight and impact to the great fiction writers and to speculate which of the masters they compare with. Thus **Adam Smith** might be considered the Homer of Economics, and his two books, 'The Wealth of Nations' and 'The Theory of Moral Sentiments', its Iliad and Odyssey. **John Maynard Keynes** can lay fair claim to be the Leo Tolstoy of the 'science' and **Alfred Marshall** perhaps its Dickens or Balzac.[4]

The behavioral/micro economists seem to belong to the more confined, microcosmic literary form of the short story. Messrs. **Thaler**, **Deaton** etc. can perhaps be considered the Chekhovs and Maupassants of Economics. Even narrower, close-focus analysis of individual behavior in economic markets like **George Akerlof**'s 'The Market for Lemons' and **Joseph Stiglitz** and **Michael Spence**'s work on asymmetric information seem like cameos. Many of the other practicing macroeconomists, churning out their pot-boiler models and theories seem more suited to the role of John Grisham or Danielle Steele (without the gripping story-lines).

Chapter 11: Notes

1. Financial Times, article, January 17th, 2017.
2. In fact plumbing, in the wider sense of large-scale interdependent hydraulic systems, was the metaphorical idea behind the impressively successful model devised by the late Wynne Godley, L. Randall Wray and the macroeconomics team

at the Levy Institute at Bard College. Godley was one of the very few to predict the Crisis of 2008.

3. However, the prudential monetary principle enunciated by Fed Chairman William McChesney Martin in the 1950s – '[The duty of central banks is to] take away the punchbowl before the party gets out of hand' - can stand as the only reliable sovereign axiom of central bank macroeconomic policy.

4. Match other notable figures from economic history with corresponding literary persons; the scope for imaginative and entertaining comparison is wide. Who is Literature's Minsky or Economics' Kafka, Borges, Proust or Joyce?

Chapter 12

WHERE DO WE GO FROM HERE?
- BACK TO THE FUTURE

PART 1: ECONOMICS AND SOCIETY:
BACK TO THE REAL WORLD

Engagement with the real world and the welfare of real human beings rather than abstract pseudo-creatures is, at last, in various ways, starting to play an important role in Economics. A few economists (Keynes is the supreme example) have always worked in the intellectual and moral territory between Economics and Politics but the most interesting and relevant economic thinking is now moving decisively into this domain. It may be too early to proclaim a revolution but there are unmistakable signs of a fundamental shift. Social and moral factors were natural concerns of early economic thinking and this development marks the return of Economics to social roots which it has systematically ignored for more than two centuries and should never have forgotten.

Adam Smith's dictum - 'It is not from the benevolence of the butcher, the brewer, or the baker that we expect our dinner, but from their regard to their own interest'[1,2] – has become famous as the social and moral justification of the free market principle which has dominated economic thinking and economic policy for the last 250 years. From its start in the now developed economies to the recent experience of emerging economies across the globe, the free market principle has very successfully delivered economic growth in a desirable, self-reinforcing virtuous circle, producing ever greater employment, social stability and the spread of wealth.

For a long while this strong, long-standing nexus has been an article of faith – an apparently natural law of Economics and the golden key to a continuous expansion of human welfare. This hitherto reliable correlation now seems to be eroding, even perhaps terminally, under the pressures of the automated production and delivery of goods and services enhanced by artificial intelligence.

In the history of human social relationships, however, the adoption of free market capitalism as the dominant economic structure constituted a seismic moral and social shift; at a stroke it reduced men from individual human agents to a mere commodity. Socially and morally it was a monumental break with the past. The social history of the early years of the Industrial Revolution in the UK records the angry reactions of the laboring classes to the new, crushing and dehumanizing force of market capital. **Karl Polanyi**'s great work, **The Great Transformation,** describes, explains and criticizes this shift in thorough detail.

Nonetheless, during the last 250 years the enormous beneficial effects of compound economic growth deriving from the spread of free market capitalism have encouraged a near-universal disregard of, and indifference to, the dehumanizing effects of the undiluted operation of the free market principle. Signs that the historical correlation between the returns to capital and the returns to labor may have reached its end are borne out by the growing social unrest in many of the developed economies. The supporting statistical evidence of this trend is very strong[3].

∿

PART 2: THE RETURN OF MORALITY IN MACROECONOMICS

The shift towards fully recognizing moral, human and social concerns as necessary factors in macroeconomics is evident in the work of several present thinkers who, like Keynes, inhabit the territory between

Economics and moral philosophy. Their work has focused on several concepts.

- **Moral Obligation and Fairness**

One factor is a growing attention to the impact on economic behavior of moral obligation, deriving from concepts of justice or from the various bonds arising from personal relationships. None of these universal and powerful human motives is addressed in the existing models of macroeconomists.

Amartya Sen has focused from the start of his career on these aspects of welfare Economics. His most recent major work, **'The Idea of Justice'**, argues persuasively in favor of the essential importance in economic behavior of the concept of fairness (which has been shown to be innate in human beings - even small children), rejecting the view, dominant in macroeconomic theory, that men are solely driven chiefly by unqualified self-interest.[4]

Michael Sandel, the moral philosopher, in his books **'Justice'** and **'What Money Can't Buy'**, uses moral concepts such as justice as critical yardsticks for measuring and assessing the social and human value of economic structures and policies.[5]

- **Community**

A different powerful impulse which mainstream macroeconomics entirely ignores is the social concept of community. To what extent, if their theories and recommendations are to be genuinely useful, should economists take into account the sense of obligation and duty arising from membership of a community? **Raghuram Rajan,** one of the very few to foresee the 2008 Crisis, regards the sense of community as a strong, natural and socially-stabilizing economic motive. Community, he maintains, is the third pillar, along with the State and the Market, in a balanced, less polarized and more effective, social and economic structure.[6]

How the sense of community actually works to sustain positive social and economic behavior in difficult conditions in the real world is the subject of a recent book by **Michael Ignatieff.**[7] With a team from the Carnegie Council for Ethics in International Affairs he visited several global hotspot neighborhoods (Jackson Heights in Queens, New York, the suburbs of Los Angeles, a favela in Rio de Janeiro, Sarajevo in Bosnia, Myanmar and others). He discovered that what enabled the diverse inhabitants of these troubled communities to achieve workable co-existence and a sense of mutual commitment was what he calls the ordinary virtues - trust, tolerance and an acceptance of the principle of human rights. For Ignatieff these virtues constitute what he calls a moral operating system which, his visits showed, has become global.

• Inequality

Another social factor attracting attention is the impact of inequality. Since the start of the Great Moderation in the early 1980s wealth inequality in the developed economies, as measured by the Gini coefficient, has soared: the rich have got significantly richer and the poor poorer. The French economist **Thomas Piketty**, in his recent book '**Capital in the Twenty-First Century**', has sought to measure the history of wealth inequality from the pre-industrial age to its recent resurgence. There have been criticisms of his method and conclusions but his book sold in the millions and has reinforced the return of social and political considerations to economic thinking and policy.

The Common Factor: a Break with the Past and a Return to Humanity

What all these thinkers share is an engagement with the strong social and moral motives of human beings as important factors in economic behavior. This is entirely new and a decisive break with the past; it distinguishes their approach decisively from the abstract mathematics which has dominated macroeconomists for the last 70 years. For all of them the abstract theorizing which has been the defining characteristic of the prevailing macroeconomic approach is empty, unrealistic and above all of little real human value.

PART 3: NEW ECONOMIC THINKING

Another positive development has been the launch of the **Institute for New Economic Thinking** (INET), with **Adair Turner** as Chairman of the Governing Board. This body was set up in October, 2009, by founders including George Soros. Its Governing and Advisory Boards comprise a roll-call of eminent personalities including economists, economic thinkers and commentators, central bankers and investment strategists.

It remains to be seen whether this intellectually and professionally well-endowed group can overcome the inertia of the dominant macroeconomic orthodoxy. In spite of the magnitude of the Crisis and its disastrous global consequences, the conduct of monetary policy since the Crisis gives no indication that the macroeconomic theory and the economic management policies which lay at its heart will be forsaken, or even critically revised, by the Federal Reserve and the other major central banks.[8,9]

However, there are encouraging signs that this new group is prepared to engage seriously with the real world. The Institute has launched an initiative 'to find solutions to what they see as the disfunctioning market economy'. This new body is called the **Commission on Global Economic Transformation**. The core areas the Commission addresses include, besides slow growth in the advanced economies and the inadequacies of the financial system, such problems as climate change, widening inequality and migration. The Commission's Board includes not only academic economists and finance officials from outside the G7 (China, Singapore, Brazil, Indonesia) but, for example, the executive director of **Oxfam**.

The Institute is also addressing the problem of the irrelevance of the traditional academic Economics curriculum. Economics faculties in a number of global universities are collaborating to devise courses which grapple with the problems facing the global economy, including inequality and global warming, rather than simply reiterating standard abstract theory.

Student Revolution

The fresh approach evidenced by the program of INET is just one item in a much wider movement to rethink from the ground up the entire structure and thrust of academic Economics courses. An editorial in the FT, 'Economics Needs to Reflect a Post-Crisis World' (September 26th, 2014), approved the shift.

Much of the impetus for these new initiatives has come from students questioning the content and whole purpose of the Economics courses they are taking and expressing forcefully their dissatisfaction with the standard curriculum.[10] **John Kay**, who is a Board member of INET, discussed in the FT (May 20th, 2014) the walk-out by students from an introductory Economics course given by Gregory Mankiw at Harvard. In April, 2014, a student group at Manchester University published a

60-page manifesto calling for substantial reform of Economics education, with a foreword by Andy Haldane of the Bank of England.[11,12,13]

~~~

PART 4: WILL THERE BE ANOTHER CRISIS?

Both **Mervyn King** and **Adair Turner**, with extensive first-hand experience of the Crisis at the highest level in central banking and finance, expect another crisis. For King the danger arises from the enormous and persistent disequilibrium in the present structure of the global economy - a disequilibrium which the dominant macroeconomic orthodoxy refused to admit was possible. Turner's concerns focus on the enormous levels of public and private debt in the global economy. He identifies as a major cause of the Crisis the blindness of the Fed's Dynamic Stochastic General Equilibrium economic model to the role of credit and finance in the economy. For him, as long as this model dominates official thinking, policy will be badly flawed.

Besides these two, **Steve Keen**, a practicing economist and one of the very few wise men who foresaw the Crisis, also expects another crisis. For him, as for Turner and King, the overriding problem facing the global economy is the level of debt. He reminds us that the level of private debt in most of the developed economies is not only the highest since the Second World War but is at a level unprecedented in the history of capitalism. He finds persuasive the already-noted analysis of **Richard Koo**, in his book '**The Holy Grail of Macroeconomics: Lessons from Japan's Great Recession**', that excessive debt, like that presently overhanging the developed economies, condemns them to persistent stagnation. Until this debt overhang is lifted or significantly reduced, growth will remain, at best, at the dismally low level it has recorded since the Crisis.

If excessive debt was a purely private problem, there would be scope for governments to adopt monetary and fiscal measures, including increasing their own debt, to stimulate their economies, encouraging growth and enabling a gradual reduction in the level of private debt. Unfortunately this ammunition was fully exhausted in the measures taken to offset the effects of the 2008 Crisis. The present level of government debt in most of the developed economies now approaches or exceeds 100% of GDP. At the IMF/Peterson Conference on Rethinking Macroeconomic Policy held in Washington in October 2017, Robert Rubin, speaking from his direct experience as Treasury Secretary in the Clinton administration, underlined the dangerous impact of excess government debt on the confidence of business managers.[14]

Keen believes that the solution to the overwhelming debt overhanging the global economy will be, in one form or another, a debt jubilee - the cancellation and/or forgiveness of enough of the present debt burden to enable a return to reasonable growth. In the absence of a widespread agreement to reduce debt via a jubilee Keen expects another Great Depression.[15]

～～～

PART 5: WHERE DO WE GO FROM HERE ?

'Where do we go from here? The only honest answer is: nobody knows.'
Alan Blinder, After the Music Stopped, 2013.

'Over the last 30 years politicians and bureaucrats the world over have come to regard economic theory as the sole source of wisdom about the manner in which a modern society should be governed. The ascendancy of economic theory has not made the world a better place.' **Steve Keen, Debunking Economics**, 2011.

'The political problem of mankind is to combine three things: economic efficiency, social justice and individual liberty.' **John Maynard Keynes.**

The 25 years of the Golden Age of Growth came to a shattering end in the global Crisis of 2008. We are still suffering from its aftermath, with widespread low growth and economic stagnation. Debt, both public and private, stands at record levels and continues to increase. The monetary policies adopted during and after the Crisis have generated a sustained boom in the price of investment assets and real estate while economic stagnation has seen real wage levels fall. The consequence has been a marked increase in social inequality and it is not difficult to see this as the major cause of the gathering social unrest in developed economies.

During the years of growth, with the strong encouragement of the Economics profession, uncritical confidence in the 'science' of Economics and in the competence of economists grew to become a generally-accepted article of faith. This credulity is still universally widespread among economists, by whom of course it is supported enthusiastically. Its persistence is given further support by the Nobel Economics Prize and the global publicity it attracts.

Unfortunately, and much more importantly, the problem is that this suspension of critical thinking remains widespread among politicians and the general public. The first sentence of the second quotation at the head of this section describes a state of affairs which essentially remains valid today, nine years after it was written and after the disastrous economic policies which led to the Crisis of 2008.

Economists as a group and Economics as a profession are still treated with a regard and respect which are thoroughly undeserved. Leading economists continue to be given space in serious journals like the

Financial Times to utter their musings on the condition of global and national economies and their recommendations for future policy. It would, as a minimum, be appropriate and welcome to see from macro-economists and from the public servants in central banks and finance ministries who followed their flawed advice some acknowledgement of their disastrous professional failure and an admission of responsibility for the devastation wreaked by the Crisis; even perhaps some signs of repentance. There have been none.

PART 6: THE LESSON OF THE CRISIS: BEWARE MACROECONOMISTS!

So far from being reliably useful, economists drove the global economy off a cliff in 2008. If there is one lesson to be gleaned from the comprehensive failures of the Economics profession over the last 25 years it is that Economics is **NOT** a reliable science. In truth economists are no better than witchdoctors and shamans. Politicians, central bankers, finance ministers and, most of all, the general public should cease forthwith to run the enormous and dangerous risk of listening passively to economists and uncritically accepting their advice.

The Last Word

Let us leave the last word to the great **Walter Bagehot**, author of the central bankers' operational manual: 'No-one, in his secret soul, was ever sorry for the death of a political economist.'[16]

Chapter 12: Notes

1. Adam Smith, An Enquiry into the Causes of the Wealth of Nations, 1776.
2. It should be noted that, before writing the 'Wealth of Nations', Adam Smith had been, from 1751-64, Professor of Moral Philosophy at Glasgow University. The fruit of his career there was his earlier work, 'The Theory of Moral Sentiments',

published in 1759-62. In this work he sought to identify the origin of man's moral sense. His conclusion was that men have a natural sympathy for their fellow human beings and that this sympathy is the origin of man's sense of morality and justice. The increasing shift in recent economic thinking towards the study of economic relationships based on moral considerations is therefore a return to original roots.

3. In the USA, for example, recent statistics from the Bureau of Labor Statistics show that over the last five decades real average middle class wages have declined by approximately 11%, even as wealth inequality has continued to soar. See: https://advisorperspectives.com/dshort/updates/2019/11/21/five-decades-of-middle-class-wages-October-2019-update.

4. See Amartya Sen, The Idea of Justice, 2009, Chapter 2, Rawls and Beyond.

5. Michael Sandel, Justice, 2010; What Money Can't Buy, 2012.

6. Raghuram Rajan, The Third Pillar, 2019.

7. Michael Ignatieff, The Ordinary Virtues – Moral Order in a Divided World, 2019.

8. John Dizard, in an article in the FT (October 2nd, 2017) prophesied 'Five years on from now, the Dynamic Stochastic General Equilibrium model that central bankers worship like Baal will still be there.'

9. This prediction has received surprising ratification from the publication in November, 2018 by Joseph Stiglitz of a long paper (number 23795) in the National Bureau of Economic Research Working Papers series. As noted earlier, it is a curious document. Stiglitz begins by giving a thorough criticism of the serious fallacies of the DSGE model (equilibrium, representative agent, absence of credit factor, simplification/reduction) but the second half of the paper is devoted to presenting a classic abstract DSGE model embellished with additional bells and whistles.

10. The Crisis seems to have encouraged rather than depressed student interest in Economics. According to an article in the FT (November 13th, 2013) the number of students taking Economics 'A' level (the high school pre-college exam in the UK) had risen by more than 50% since 2007.

11. 'Education and Unlearning: Education at the University of Manchester. Report available through their website: http://www.post-crasheconomics.com.

12. There is also some limited evidence that the real world, in the form of empirical evidence, is starting to play a role in academic Economics. According to Dani Rodrik, in his book 'Economics Rules', published in 2015, 'it is virtually impossible to publish in top journals …. without including some serious empirical analysis.' He is referring only to development and international economics but the award of the 2019 Nobel Economics Prize for the successful development and application of randomized controlled trials in some areas of social policy is confirmation of the growing, overdue and welcome impact of empiricism in Economics.

13. Courses on economic history are also making a long-overdue and deserved comeback.

14. It is worth recalling that, with the exception of the British recovery from the debt of the Napoleonic Wars thanks to the growth generated by the Industrial Revolution, every single instance of excess debt has ultimately been 'resolved' by inflation.

15. See his 'Can We Avoid Another Financial Crisis', 2017, and also 'Debunking Economics', Chapter 13, in which Keen sets out the debt problems facing the world's economies and banks. Keen comments that a debt jubilee would wipe out the banks and that the banker lobby team, with strong support from mainstream academic economists, would prevent it.

16. Walter Bagehot, 1858. Bagehot's actual words were: 'No English gentleman' rather than 'No-one' but the sentiment seems universally sound.

Epilogue

The Corona Virus

This book was written before the outbreak of the Corona-19 virus pandemic. The pandemic has plunged the global economy into paralysis - a paralysis which, as this epilogue is written, still seems to be in its early stages. In the developed economies, which have been the first victims of the virus, the immediate effects have already been devastating. In effect, for most of the affected countries, the entire economy has suddenly shut down, with a collapse in economic activity and soaring unemployment.

After only a few months effects are already threatening to be worse than in the Great Depression of 1929. Furthermore the probability is that the global economic devastation will get much worse. So far it is the developed economies which have borne the brunt of the disaster but it is very unlikely that the emerging and less-developed economies, with much worse organized healthcare systems, will escape similar if not worse turmoil.

In this emergency environment disputes about the relative value of competing macroeconomic theories are irrelevant. The vicious speed and extent of the economic collapse has forced governments to turn to the only immediate potential remedy available to them - monetary injection on a massive scale - as the quickest means of offsetting the slump in consumption and the threat of immediate wholesale destitution.

This has meant an explosion in government deficits and, since companies and individuals in the process of failure or bankruptcy do not pay taxes, will lead to a massive rise in government debt. So-called Modern Monetary Theory (essentially: governments can safely borrow almost unlimited amounts in their own currency without bad consequences) will receive a baptism of fire and an immediate test, perhaps to destruction.

Also, when we finally emerge from the threat of the virus, it is extremely unlikely that there will be a simple return to the free market/ economic-growth-at-all-costs paradigm. In fact, since scientists think that this pandemic is likely to be only the first of many, the great probability is that the fundamental economic structure and operation of our societies will have to alter to accommodate new and pressing factors: lower consumption and lower growth, more secure (ideally domestic and probably much more costly) supply structures, an acceptance of more socially-equitable, reasonably comfortable but not luxurious existence (farewell to the Financial Times 'How to Spend It' weekend extravagances) and, let us hope, a much better mutually sustaining relationship with the natural world.

Nonetheless, the skeptical criticism this book has levelled at macroeconomics and its practitioners remains valid. Indeed, the new 'normal' will require undiminished vigilance as to the real value of the Economics profession and of economic experts.

Bibliography

Akerlof, George and Shiller, Robert. *Animal Spirits.* (Princeton University Press, 2009).

Akerlof, George and Others. *What Have We Learned ?* (IMF and MIT Press, 2014).

Appelbaum, Binyamin. *The Economists' Hour.* (Little, Brown & Company, 2019).

Baumol, William and Blinder, Alan. *Macroeconomics: Principles and Policy.* (Cengage, 2010 and others).

Bernanke, Ben. *The Courage to Act.* (W.W. Norton, 2015).

Blanchard, Olivier and Others. *Evolution or Revolution?: Rethinking Macroeconomic Policy after the Great Recession.* (MIT Press, 2019).

Blanchard, Olivier and Others. *In the Wake of the Crisis.* (IMF, 2012).

Blanchard, Olivier. *Macroeconomics.* (Pearson Education Limited, 2017).

Blanchard, Olivier and Others. *Progress and Confusion: the State of Macroeconomic Policy.* (IMF, 2016).

Blaug, Mark. *The Methodology of Economics.* (Cambridge University Press, 1980).

Blinder, Alan. *After the Music Stopped.* (Penguin Press, 2013).

Boland, Lawrence. *Model Building in Economics.* (Cambridge University Press, 2014).

Bookstaber, Richard. *A Demon of Our Own Design.* (John Wiley, 2007).

Bookstaber, Richard. *The End of Theory* (Princeton University Press, 2017).

Buchanan, James M. and Tullock, Gordon. *The Calculus of Consent.* (University of Michigan Press, 1965).

Chang, Ha Joon. *Economics: the User's Guide.* (Penguin Books, 2014).

Coase, Ronald. *Essays on Economics and Economists.* (University of Chicago Press, 1994).

Coyle, Diane, *GDP, a Brief but Affectionate History.* (Princeton University Press, 2014).

Datta, Saugato (editor). *Economics: Making Sense of the Modern Economy.* (The Economist/Profile Books, 2011).

Derman, Emanuel. *Models Behaving Badly.* (Free Press, 2011).

Dumas, Charles. *Globalisation Fractures.* (Profile Books, 2010).

Fisher, Irving. *The Debt Deflation Theory of Great Depressions.* (ThaiSunset Publications. 2010).

Galbraith, John Kenneth. *A Short History of Financial Euphoria.* (Penguin Books, 1994).

Greenspan, Alan. *The Map and the Territory.* (The Penguin Press, 2013).

Gagnon, Joseph and Hinterschweiger, Marc. *The Global Outlook for Government Debt over the Next 25 Years.* (Peterson Institute, 2011).

Godley, Wynne and Marc Lavoie. *Monetary Economics: An Integrated Approach to Credit, Money, Income, Production and Wealth.* (Palgrave, MacMillan, 2007).

Hausman, Daniel (editor). *The Philosophy of Economics.* (Cambridge University Press, 1994).

Hicks, John. *Causality in Economics.* (Basic Books, 1979).

Ignatieff, Michael. *The Ordinary Virtues – Moral Order in a Divided World.* (Harvard University Press, 2019).

Kahneman, Daniel. *Thinking, Fast and Slow.* (Farrar, Strauss and Giroux, 2011).

Karier, Thomas. *Intellectual Capital: Forty Years of the Nobel Prize in Economics.* (Cambridge University Press, 2010).

Kay, John. *Obliquity.* (Profile Books, 2010).

Keen, Steve. *Can We Have Another Crisis?* (Polity Press, 2017).

Keen, Steve. *Debunking Economics.* (Zed Books, 2011).

Keynes, John Maynard. *The General Theory of Employment, Interest and Money.* (Palgrave Macmillan, 1936).

Kindleberger, Charles. *Comparative Political Economy.* (MIT Press, 2000).

Kindleberger, Charles. *Manias, Panics and Crashes.* (John Wiley, 2005).

King, Mervyn. *The End of Alchemy.* (W.W. Norton, 2016).

Koo, Richard. *The Holy Grail of Macroeconomics.* (John Wiley, 2008).

Levitt, Steven and Dubner, Stephen. *Freakonomics.* (HarperCollins, 2005).

Levitt, Steven and Dubner, Stephen. *Superfreakonomics* (HarperCollins, 2009).

Madrick, Jeff. *Seven Bad Ideas.* (Alfred Knopf, 2014).

Mallaby, Stephen. *The Man who Knew.* (Penguin Press, 2016).

Mankiw, N. Gregory. *Principles of Macroeconomics.* (Cengage, 2012, and others).

Marshall, Alan. *Principles of Economics.* (Macmillan, 1920).

McCarthy, Stephen and Kehl, David. *Deductive Irrationality.* (Lexington Books, 2008).

McCloskey, Deirdre. *The Secret Sins of Economics.* (Prickly Paradigm Press, 2002).

Minsky, Hyman. *Can It Happen Again?* (M. E. Sharpe, 1982).

Minsky, Hyman. *Stabilizing an Unstable Economy.* (Yale University Press, 1986).

Mirowski, Philip. *Never Let a Serious Crisis Go to Waste.* (Verso, 2014).

Morgenstern, Oskar. *On the Accuracy of Economic Observations.* (Princeton University Press, 1965).

Morris, Charles. *The Two Trillion Dollar Meltdown.* (Perseus Books Group, 2008).

Offer, Avner and Soderberg, Gabriel. *The Nobel Factor* (Princeton University Press, 2016).

Olson, Mancur. *Power and Prosperity.* (Basic Books, 2000).

Piketty, Thomas. *Capitalism in the 21st Century.* (Harvard College Press, 2014).

Polanyi, Karl. *The Great Transformation.* (Farrar & Rinehart, 1944; Beacon Press Books, 1957, 2001).

Quiggin, John. *Zombie Economics.* (Princeton University Press, 2010).

Rajan, Raghuram. *Fault Lines.* (Princeton University Press, 2010).

Rajan, Raghuram. *The Third Pillar.* (Harper, Collins, 2019).

Rand, Ayn. *Atlas Shrugged.* (Penguin Press, 1957).

Rand, Ayn. *Introduction to Objectivist Epistemology.* (Penguin Press, 1966).

Rand, Ayn. *The Virtue of Selfishness.* (New American Library, 1961).

Reinhart, Carmen and Rogoff, Kenneth. *A Decade of Debt.* (Peterson Institute, 2011).

Robbins, Lionel. *A History of Economic Thought.* (Princeton University Press, 1998).

Robbins, Lionel. *An Essay on the Nature and Significance of Economic Science.* (Macmillan, 1932).

Robbins, Lionel. *The Evolution of Modern Economic Theory.* (Aldine Pub. Co., 1970).

Robinson, Joan. *Economic Philosophy.* (C.A.Watts, 1962).

Robinson, Joan. *Freedom and Necessity.* (George Allen and Unwin, 1970).

Rodrik, Dani. *Economics Rules: The Rights and Wrongs of the Dismal Science.* (W.W.Norton, 2015).

Roubini, Nouriel and Mihm, Stephen. *Crisis Economics.* (Penguin Press, 2010).

Sandel, Michael. *Justice: What's the Right Thing to Do?* (Farrar, Straus and Giroux, 2010).

Sandel, Michael. *Liberalism and the Limits of Justice.* (Cambridge University Press, 1982).

Sandel, Michael. *What Money Can't Buy.* (Farrar, Straus and Giroux, 2012).

Schabas, Margaret. *A World Ruled by Numbers: William Stanley Jevons and the Rise of Mathematical Economics.* (Princeton University Press, 1990).

Sen, Amartya. *Rationality and Freedom.* (Harvard University Press, 2002).

Sen, Amartya. *On Economic Inequality.* (Oxford University Press, 1997).

Sen, Amartya. *The Idea of Justice.* (Harvard University Press, 2009).

Simon, Herbert. *Reason in Human Affair.* (Stanford University Press, 1981).

Smith, Adam. *An Inquiry into the Nature and Causes of the Wealth of Nations.* (1776).

Smith, Adam. *The Theory of Moral Sentiments.* (1759-62).

Stein, Herbert. *What I Think: Essays on Economics, Politics and Life.* (AEI Press, 1998).

Taleb, Nassim Nicholas. *The Black Swan.* (Random House, 2007).

Tetlock, Philip. *Expert Political Judgement.* (Princeton University Press, 2005).

Thaler, Richard. *Misbehaving; the Making of Behavioral Economics.* (W.W. Norton, 2015).

Thaler, Richard. *Nudge: Improving Decisions about Health, Wealth and Happiness.* (Yale University Press, 2008).

Tirole, Jean. *Economics for the Common Good.* (Princeton University Press, 2017).

Turner, Adair. *Between Debt and the Devil.* (Princeton University Press, 2016).

Turner, Adair. *Economics After the Crisis.* (MIT, 2012).

Vague, Richard. *The Next Economic Disaster.* (University of Pennsylvania Press, 2014).

Varoufakis, Yanis. *Adults in the Room.* (The Bodley Head/Farrar, Strauss and Giroux, 2017).

Varoufakis, Yanis. *And the Weak Suffer What They Must?* (Nation Books, 2016).

Wapshott, Nicholas. *Keynes and Hayek: the Clash that Defined Modern Economics.* (W.W. Norton, 2011).

Wicksteed, Philip. *The Common Sense of Political Economy.* (Routledge, 2003 (reprint)).

Wiedemer, David and Others. *Aftershock.* (John Wiley, 2010).

Wolf, Martin. *The Shifts and Shocks: What We've Learned - and Have Still to Learn - from the Financial Crisis.* (Penguin Press, 2014).

INDEX

Akerlof, George, 4, 89, 99, 146-7, 154, 161, 168
All Souls College, Oxford, 162
American Economic Association, 4, 164
journals, 7-9
membership, 7
American Economic Review, 8, 78, 142, 146
American Economist, 78
American Statistical Association, membership, 9
Apollo moonshot, 156
Appelbaum, Binyamin, 127
Artifical Intelligence (AI), 92, 171
Austrian School, 103
Bagehot, Walter, 35, 179, 181
Baker, Dean, 51
Baltic Dry Index, 23, 47
Balzac, Honore de, 168
Banerjee, Abhijit, 148, 162
Bank for International Settlements (BIS), 27, 29
Bank of England, 29, 61, 71-2, 77, 164
Bank of Japan, 29, 92
banking,
credit practices, 15, 19
leverage, 14-16, 24-5
shadow-banking, 13
traditional structure, 62
VAR, 144
Barron's, 11, 99
Baumol, William, 85
BCA Research, 18
Bear Stearns, 17, 21
Becker, Gary, 147, 154
Behavioral Economics, 58, 127-8, 143, 146-8, 151, 155, 161
Bernanke, Ben, iii, 13, 20, 22, 31-3, 37-8, 42-4, 47-8, 52, 55-6, 58, 61, 116, 126, 157

Berra, Yogi, 71
Bezemer, Dirk, 53
Black Monday, 1987, 40
Blanchard, Olivier, 4, 60-1, 65, 85
Blaug, Mark, 86, 137
Blinder, Alan, 55, 57, 61, 77, 85, 177
Bloomberg TV, 5-6
BNP, 17
Bohr, Niels, 71
Boland, Lawrence, 106
Borges, Jorge Luis, 169
Borio, Claudio, 27
Born, Brooksley, 37
Boulding, Kenneth, 99
Brazil, 3, 175
Bretton Woods, 113
Broadbent, Ben, 71
bubbles, financial, 34-6, 43, 48, 50
Buffett, Warren, 145
Bureau of Economic Analysis, 69
Burns, Arthur, 1
Bush, G H W, 77
Bush, G W, 38, 77
business cycles, 91, 128
Capital Asset Pricing Model, 64
Carter, Jimmy, 1
central banks, 24, 64, 71, 135, 174
balance sheets, 29
Golden Rule, 35
operational improvements, 62
Chang, Ha-Joon, 79, 131-3, 137, 139, 166
Chekhov, Anton, 168
Cheney, Dick, 128
Chicago University, 5, 84, 116
China, 3, 134, 136, 158
Chomsky, Noam, 106
Citibank, 16-17
Clinton, Bill, 32, 38, 77
CNBC, i, 5, 15

Coase, Ronald, i, 86, 101, 121
Commission on Global Economic Transformation, 175
Commission on the Crisis, Federal iv, 20, 45, 49, 53
Commodity Futures Trading Commission (CFTC), 37
Commodity Modernization Act, 37
community, sense of, 172-3
computing power, 15
conferences, 58-61, 64, 191
Corona-19 Virus, x, 182-3
Countrywide, 19
Coyle, Diana, 90
credit crises, 34, 100, 126
credit default swaps, 41
credit expansion, 31-6, 41-4, 50, 52
Deaton, Angus, 148, 155, 168
debt, 14, 25-6, 47, 135, 176-7
  global debt supercycle, 19, 31
  jubilee, 177
dentistry, 164, 166
Depression, Great, ii, 2, 7, 14, 27, 36, 38, 44, 47, 62, 65, 103, 124, 134, 157, 177, 182
derivatives, 16-20, 32-3, 37, 41, 144
Derman, Emanuel, 106
Deutsche Bank, 17
Dickens, Charles, 168
Dizard, John, *Financial Times*, 180
DNA, discovery, 165
Dubner, Stephen, 141, 147
Dudley, William, 38
Duflo, Esther, 148, 162, 164
Dynamic Stochastic General Equilibrium model (DSGE), v, ix, 44, 46, 48, 57-8, 61, 63, 114, 119-127, 129, 176, 180
  failure of, 126-7
ECB (European Central Bank), 26, 29, 72, 77, 117, 129, 157, 159
Econometric Society, 67
Econometrica, 8
economics,
  academic curriculum, 175
  analogies for, 163-9
and the 'hard sciences', 87-9, 137-40, 149, 167
  austerity, 103, 158-160
  Austrian school, 103
  business cycles, 91
  confidence trick, 96-7
  deficit spending, 116, 128, 134-5
  degree courses, demand, 5
  elite priesthood, 95-6, 105, 112
  empirical evidence, 146-8, 180
  equilibrium, 100, 120-1, 123-4
  forecasting, 11, 48, 56, 67-77
  free-market capitalism/approach, 42-3, 114, 170-1
  history, 83-4
  instability, 123-4
  journals, 7-9, 11
  models, 46, 105-12
  neo-classical, 43, 56, 116
  novel-writing, 167-8
  orthodoxies, 112-19, 135
  plumbing, 164, 166, 168
  policy contradictions, 157
  policy presentation, 72-5
  professional associations, 7
  scientism, 160
  textbooks, 84-5
  theories, life-cycle of, 104
  T.O.E., 131-6
Economist, The, iv, 11, 34, 52, 59-60, 70-1, 77
econs and modls, 111, 127
Efficient Market Hypothesis, 58, 64
Einstein, Albert, 109,132
Elizabeth II, Queen, i,1
Elster, Jon, 153, 155
engineering, 164, 166
Engle, Robert, 154
Euro, 62, 117-8, 159
European Commission, 117, 129, 157
European Exchange Rate Mechanism (ERM), 77
Eurozone, EZ, 28, 62, 69, 103, 117, 128, 136, 157, 159-60
fairness, 172
Fama, Eugene, 154

Federal Reserve, US, ii, viii, 12, 14, 20-21, 23, 25, 29-44, 55, 57, 70, 72, 77, 91-2, 99, 124-6, 128-9, 141, 157, 174
economics staff, 57, 119
suppression of dissent, 124-6
Federal Reserve, New York, 38
Fiedler, Edgar, 68
Financial Media, 5-6
Financial Times, The, passim
Fisher, Irving, 70
Fitch, 39
Forbes Magazine, 11
foreign exchange market (f/x), 19
France, 28, 36, 117, 159
Friedman, Milton, 104, 116, 153
Friedman, Thomas, 3
Frisch, Ragnar, 154
Fukuyama, Francis, 3
Galbraith, J K, 65, 68
Galbraith, James, 129
GATT, 2
Gaussian copula, 150-1
GDP, 90-1
Geithner, Tim, 56
Germany, 69, 117-18, 134
Giles, Chris, *Financial Times,* 77
Gini coefficient, 173
Glass-Steagall Act, 13, 31, 37-9
Global Economic Transformation, Commission on, 175
Godley, Wynne, 49-51, 168-9
Goldman Sachs, 17, 19-20, 31-2, 145
gold standard, 1, 113
Goodhart, Charles, 127, 150
Granger, Clive, 93
Greece, 19-20, 28, 31, 117, 128-9
Greenspan, Alan, i, iii, 10-11, 13, 20, 22, 24, 31, 33, 37, 40-8, 52, 55-7, 61, 68, 73, 76-8, 96-7, 101, 119, 122, 126, 140-1, 143
Grisham, John, 168
Haldane, Andy, 71, 77, 164, 176
Hansen, Fred, 51
Harford, Tim, 68, 164
Harrod, Roy, 137
Harvard University, 5

Hayek, Friedrich von, 65, 88, 152-3, 160-1
Heckman, James, 154
Hensen, Lars, 154
Hicks, John, 89, 141, 150
Higgs, Peter, 88, 109, 132, 156
Hippocratic Oath, 68, 156
Homer, 168
Iliad, 168
Odyssey, 168
Hoover, H, 157
Hubbard, Glen, 38
Hubble telescope, 156
Hudson, Michael, 51
Huffington Post, 125, 129-30
Ignatieff, Michael, 173, 180
IMF, iii, 2, 4, 23, 29, 32, 40, 52, 54, 59, 64, 69, 72, 77, 103, 113-4, 129, 157-9
India, 3
Indonesia, 175
inequality, 173, 178
inertia, 97, 143
inflation, 135, 181
Institute for New Economic Thinking, 128, 174-5
interest rates, 29, 71
Italy, 28, 117
Jackson Hole, IMF Conference, 2005, 51
Japan, 28, 69, 157
Jevons, William, 98
journals, economics, 7-9
Joyce, James, 169
JSTOR, 8
Kafka, Franz, 169
Kahnemann, Daniel, 151, 154
Kaufman, Henry, 124
Kay, John, 175
Keen, Steve, 49-50, 67, 79, 86-7, 95, 99, 100, 120, 122, 129, 131, 136-7, 140-1, 176-7, 181
Kennedy, J F, 116
Keynes, John Maynard, viii, ix, 7, 8, 65, 78, 79, 81-2, 91, 101-4, 110, 113, 120, 128, 134, 137, 139, 151, 161,

163, 165, 167-8, 170-1, 178
King, Mervyn, 61-3, 176
Knight, Frank, i
Kocherlakota, Narayana, 111
Koo, Richard, 25, 176
Kremer, Michael, 148, 162
Krugman, Paul, i, iii, 22, 58, 65, 116, 162
Lagarde, Christine, 64
Law, John, 36
Lehman Brothers, 20-21, 25, 46, 63, 145
Leijonhufvud, Axel, 111, 127
Leontief, Wassily, 107
leverage, 13, 16-19, 40, 100
Levitt, Steve, 141, 147
Levy Institute/Bard College, 169
Lewis, Michael, 22
Little, Daniel, 127
London School of Economics, i, 63, 115
Long Term Capital Management (LTCM), 10, 41, 145
Lucas, Robert 4, 10, 138
Lucas critique, 127
Mackenzie, D, and Spears, T, 151
macroeconomics, 101
  cause and effect in, 158
  confidence trick, 75-6
  elite, 105
  experiments in, 133-6
  fallibility, 63-4
  Golden Age of, 4-11
  moral concepts in, 171-2
  orthodoxy, 63
  theories, life-cycle of, 104
  theories, multiplicity of, 133
Mallaby, Sebastian, 51-2, 57
Mankiw, Greg, 82-3, 85, 96, 112, 175
Marcus, Gill, 64
Marshall, Alfred, 81-2, 89, 102, 122, 168
mathematics, 79-100, 118
  and a scholar's career, 99
  corruption of economics, 94-8
  non-linear dynamic equations, 92

quantification, 88-91
Maupassant, Guy de, 168
McCain, John, 13, 78
McChesney Martin, William, 35, 52, 169
McCloskey, Deirdre, 79, 81, 83, 137, 140-1, 150
McKinsey Global Institute, 29
measurement/quantification, 88-91, 143
Mellon, Andrew, 103, 157
Micawber Mr., 28
microeconomics, 146-50
Mill, John Stuart, 81, 106
Minsky, Hyman, 44, 51, 123-5, 129, 169
Mirowski, Paul, 22
Mises Institute, 116
Mises, Ludwig von, 103
MIT, 4, 5
models, i, 46, 93, 106-12
  size, 127
Moderation, Great, 4-5, 10, 15, 20, 48, 100, 115, 126, 136, 144, 173
Modern Monetary Theory, 182-3
monetarism, 115-6
Montier, James (GMO), 99
Moody's, 39
Moore's Law, 2, 14
moral obligation, 172
mortgage finance market, 43
Morgan Stanley, 17, 28
Morrison, Charles, 29, 51
muggles, 79, 82, 96
Myrdal, Gunnar, 153
NAIRU, 115
N.B.E.R., 3, 129
New York Times, The, iv, 64, 162
Nixon, Richard, 1, 113
Nobel, Alfred, 155
Nobel Prize in Economics, iii, ix, 149, 152-62, 178
novel-writing, 167-8
OECD, 27, 29
Offer, Avner, 152, 161
Orwell, George, 112, 126

Oxfam, 3, 175
PBS Frontline 22
penicillin, 165
Peterson Institute, 59-60
Phelps, Edmund, 98, 100
Phillips Curve, 104, 115
Pigou A C, 8
Piketty, Thomas, 173
Plender, John, *Financial Times*, 122
plumbing, 164, 166, 168
Polanyi, Karl, i, 171
Portugal, 28, 117
poverty, extreme, 3, 13
Prince, Chuck, Citibank, 16-17
Princeton University, 5
Proust, Marcel, 169
quantification/measurement, 88-91, 143
quantitative easing (QE), 27-9, 157-8
Rajan, Raghuram, 49-51, 172, 180
Rand, Ayn, 43, 52-3
  Atlas Shrugged, 53
  The Fountainhead, 53
rating agencies, 14, 39-40
Recession, Great, 115, 157
regression analysis, 48, 140-1
regulation, 36-8, 45
risk,
  and uncertainty, 144-5
  interdependency, 18
  market volatility, 144
  models, 16-19
Robbins, Lionel, 8
Robinson, Joan, 65, 93
Rodrik, Dani, 95, 105-11, 133-4, 166-7, 180
Romer, Paul, viii, 52, 76, 78, 97-8
Roosevelt, Franklin, 52,116
Roth, Al, 164
Roubini, Nuriel, 49-50
Rubin, Robert, iii, 10, 31-2, 37, 49, 177
Russia/USSR, iv, 2-3, 134, 136, 158
Samuelson, Paul, 4, 80, 84-5, 87, 139, 154
Sandel, Michael, 172, 180

Schiff, Peter, 51
Schumpeter, Joseph, 80, 99
Sen, Amartya, 172, 180
shamans/witchdoctors, vii, ix, 161, 179
Shiller, Robert, ix, 4, 49-50, 89, 99, 154, 164
Shilling, Gary, 51
sigma/price volatility, 144-5
Simon, Herbert, 151
Singapore, 175
Smith, Adam, 81, 106, 121, 168, 170, 179-80
Smith, Vernon, 151
Smoot-Hawley Act, 2
Societe Generale, 19, 31
Soderberg, Gabriel, 152, 161
Solow, Robert, 154
Sorkin, Andrew Ross, 22, 58
Soros, George, 19, 174
South Sea Bubble, 34, 36
Spain, 117
Spence, Michael, 147, 154, 161, 168
stagnation, 69
  secular, 25
Standard & Poor's, 39
statistics, 9, 96-7, 140-5
  statistical significance, 9, 142-4
Steele, Danielle, 168
Stein, Herb, 68
Stiglitz, Joseph, iii, 116, 120, 129, 147, 154, 161-2, 168, 180
stockmarkets, 4, 13
  US, 11, 40-1, 57, 70
Sugden, Robert, 106
Summers, Lawrence, iii, 10, 25, 31-2, 37-8, 42, 55, 60, 91, 98, 126, 162
swans, black, 145
Taleb, Nassim Nicholas, 121, 145, 151-2
Tetlock, Philip, 67, 138
Tett, Gillian, *Financial Times*, 20
Thaler, Richard, 80, 128, 143, 146-8, 155, 168
TIME magazine, iv, 10
Tinbergen, Jan, 154
Tirole, Jean, 148

Tolstoy, Leo, 168
Treasury, US, 30, 34, 46-7, 55, 67, 126, 157
tulip mania, 34
Turner, Adair, 63, 174, 176
UK, 28, 36, 136
uncertainty and risk, 144-5
UNCTAD, 3
US unemployment, 11, 23
VAR, 144
Varoufakis, Yanis, 99, 128
Venezuela, 134, 136
Viniar, David, Citibank, 145
volatility, 144-5
Volcker, Paul, 1
Voyager Spacecraft, 156, 165
Wall Street Journal, The, 11, 70
Walras, Leon, 98-9, 107, 121

Weimar Republic, 134
White, William, 49-50, 52, 64
witchdoctors/shamans, vii, ix, 161, 179
Wolf, Martin, 44, 52, 55
World Bank, iii,19, 30, 72
world trade, 12, 23, 69
World Trade Organization (WTO), 2, 69
Wray, L. Randall, 168
Wright Brothers, 156
Yahoo, 6
Yale University, 5
Yellen, Janet, 99, 116
Young, Roy, 52
Zakaria, Fareed, 98, 100
Zimbabwe, 134, 136
zombie companies/economies, 26-7